How to Manage
Your Money
When You
Don't Have Any

Second Edition

Erik Wecks

Table of Contents

Preface to the Second Edition

Wow! I'm not really sure what else to say. The response to the first edition of *How to Manage Your Money When You Don't Have Any* has far exceeded my hopes and dreams. I am truly grateful to know that over 60,000 families have benefited from the book. That still blows my mind.

A lot has changed since the fall of 2011 when I wrote the first edition. In just over three-and-a-half years, our economy has improved drastically. Employment finally looks like it has turned around. There are hints the some of the long-term unemployed may be reentering the workforce.

Even so, some of the underlying structure remains the same. Wages are just starting to rise, and many families still live month to month. More ominously to me, personal debt is growing again in the United States. It currently sits at $860,000,000,000. That's eight hundred and sixty billion dollars for those of you who didn't count the zeros. More interestingly, the debt is concentrated in fewer households, with the percentage of households using personal debt products about 10 percent lower than it was in 2008. So while some of us learned our lesson, there are still a whole lot of families who prefer enriching the bankers instead of themselves.

There's still lots of work to do. If this is your first time reading *How to Manage Your Money When You Don't Have Any* you may hear echoes of a darker time in the text. I think that's a good thing. When I went to revise the text, I found that even I had forgotten how difficult the Great Recession had been for me personally. During the dark years, I survived three career changes without losing my home. The principles of this book will show you how that was even possible.

I know that such hard times may feel far away for many of you—a memory best left buried. Now is the time to get ready—to prepare for the next fiscal meltdown. For even if the dark days are now sunny—and thank goodness they are— wisdom is often found in a voice from a different time. This book can teach you to keep your eye on the ball before the next recession makes it difficult for us all.

It's not just the economy that has improved in the last few years. My writing style has also changed quite a bit. For one thing, I haven't written much non-fiction until recently. As I started reading back through the text of the first edition, I was worried that I would cringe as I read my work. Instead, I was pleasantly surprised how well it had held up. Oh there were grammar problems and convoluted sentences, but I think much of the success of the first edition came from its personable style and my story. It's a relatable book, and that's something that I didn't want to remove from the text. That said, the section on "strategies" needed a complete reorganization. The changes in that section were extensive, although the content remained largely the same. In a few places, some of the information felt a little dated. For example, the information on what to do when you get behind on your mortgage was completely out of date. In late 2011, the banks were just beginning to responsibly manage their backlog of delinquent owners. Since then, the post recession refinance options have widened significantly. So the section on falling behind was rewritten.

Perhaps the most significant changes came from Kay Moore, a friend and editor who gave the book a thorough scrubbing. You owe Kay a huge debt of gratitude for taking a book of worthwhile content and frustrating errors and turning it into something much less irritating. Thank you Kay.

I hope *How to Manage Your Money When You Don't Have Any* helps you as it has so many others. I'm looking forward to the next few years of economic improvement and to hearing your success stories.

Erik Wecks
March 2015
Vancouver, WA

Preface to the First Edition

Since the beginning of the Great Recession, gallons of ink have been spilled trying to create cosmic justice for past sins and present economic inequities. For those of us damaged by the disaster, much of that passion feels like wasted time and energy. This isn't one of those books. This book is for the disheartened reader who, for whatever reason, is having trouble remembering their life before they felt financially out of control. While this book offers no solutions to make corporations behave like decent, ethical "people," it does offer a simple, clear path toward a more stable financial existence for those willing to accept it.

Readers of all income levels can find its simple financial plan useful. However, since this book focuses on doing your very best with your current income, readers looking for discussions on long-term planning or investments might be disappointed. Don't misunderstand: long-term planning is vital for financial stability, but there are so many other great books on the topic we won't deal with those topics here. So if your concerns revolve around what will happen to your child's financial aid when you gift them a large portfolio of stocks, this book may have little to offer you.

On the other hand, if your concerns revolve around how to make sure you can afford to pay the mortgage on an upside down house so your child has a roof over their head, this book is for you.

If you have read other personal finance books, I hope you aren't disappointed to find this one a little different. Many, but not all, personal finance books offer what I call the bowl-of-popcorn approach to financial advice. They are full of little chewy nuggets of information that may or may not be useful on a daily basis. Very few of them offer a single coherent financial plan integrated throughout the book. Notable exceptions exist; my aim is to be among them.

For the author, the risk with aiming a little higher than popcorn advice is that I may lose my audience along the way. A book of popcorn is safe because just about everyone can find something useful in such a book. Everyone goes home a winner, and no one gets hurt. But nuggets of advice have very little power to comfort us or assist us if we are experiencing any serious financial problems. In order to help households truly suffering from the effects of the Great Recession, I will have to ask for something from my readers, and so I risk alienating many of them.

If you are going to benefit from this book, you and I will have to agree that lasting change takes more than simply changing what you *do*. Lasting change also requires that you alter what you *believe* about money. To me, changing what you *do* without changing what you *believe* is very similar to dieting. The weight comes off, but unless you come to *believe* that healthy foods can satisfy your cravings better than junk food, the diet won't work. As soon as your diet ends, you'll go right back to eating the way you ate before and end up putting the weight back on. The same holds true with financial changes. I can teach you how to avoid impulse purchases at the grocery store, but that won't help you if your belief system about money is broken. You will just impulse buy online instead.

Remember, your values and choices have caused or at least contributed to your stress. Are you ready to try something different? In our house we have a saying, two plus two always equals four. If you believe and do the same things you did in the past, you will get the same results in the future. So if I am going to help you, I have to ask you to think critically about how you have dealt with money in the past and adopt new ways of thinking about it in the present. These new ways of thinking will form the foundation that will help you benefit from the nuts-and-bolts practical advice I will give you later in the book. If you read with an open mind, it will be worth the wait.

The plan I offer isn't pie-in-the-sky idealism either. This is the battle-hardened financial plan that has guided my family for years. It is also the same plan I preached to other families as a real estate agent, financial adviser, and financial counselor. The benefit I've received from following this plan are emotional for me. I've survived and I have this financial plan to thank for it. Through my own experience, I know that the information in this book can change the way you deal with money and relieve your stress.

To start, we need to peek out of our foxhole and take a look around. It's time for a short assessment of the financial landscape we find ourselves facing as a country. Our collective thinking and actions created it, and now we as individuals have to live with it. Along the way, I will tell you more of my story and introduce the concept that will organize our financial plan throughout the book.

**Workbook Available
May 15, 2015**

HOW TO MANAGE

YOUR MONEY

WHEN YOU

DON'T HAVE ANY

Workbook

ERIK WECKS

How to Manage
Your Money
When You
Don't Have Any

Chapter 1:
Houston, We Have a
Problem...

In the fall of 2011 when I first sat down to write a personal finance book for those who struggled to get by on a month-to-month basis, things looked pretty grim. While the US unemployment rate had finally started to fall in recent months, it would take three years of consistent job growth to bring us to a place where things started to feel normal. Besides, actual unemployment was likely much higher than reported, because government unemployment numbers only count those actively looking for work. An unknown number of additional workers had given up. At the time, the federal Bureau of Labor Statistics estimated only 66 percent of working-age males were currently employed. Working-age male employment had been declining for decades, but the 2008 recession pushed it off a cliff. If you were so unfortunate as to become unemployed, it took an average of 40 weeks to find employment. Some argued, long-term unemployment numbers were similar or worse than those during Great Depression of the 1930's. It was a dark time.

Now, in the winter of 2015, the unemployment rate has dropped steeply. More interestingly, the labor participation rate has continued to drop. It now sits at just under 63 percent. It remains a matter of strong debate as to why the participation rate continues to drop. However, I think it's safe to say that, in general, things feel a little better, economically, but it's a different kind of better. For many, it's a two jobs just to make ends meet kind of better. It's a twenty-four-year-old child living with parents while working part time to pay student debt kind of better.

Defining the Problem

It would be easy to pull a simple writer's trick at this point. I could tell you what I call an Eden story. An Eden story is a story about the idyllic time before the beginning of our troubles. The trick works well because it resonates so powerfully within most of us. Most human beings seem to long for a time before innocence was lost. Isn't this how many fiction stories begin? There is a short time of peace that sets the stage for the conflict. In this case, the story could start in the time before we came to be controlled by big bad personal debt. All I have to do is pick a significant decade, say the 1930s, and tell you how most people from that era felt being in debt was evil and how they worked hard to avoid all debt. Then comes the fall from grace, the moment we "sinned" as a people and our troubles began. In this case, the role could be played by the post-World War II housing boom led by the new FHA mortgages. I could talk about the terrible compromises of the so-called "greatest generation," how it was their Diners Club Card that introduced our culture to easy debt and made it prestigious. I could tell you this story, but beware. Like most Eden stories, it isn't the whole truth. In particular, there just hasn't been a time in our culture or any other culture that pre-dates debt.

Oh, yes, views about debt have changed over time, and I, of course, would like to change your views about debt, but personal debt has a much longer, richer, and more interesting history in our world than our problems in the present. Debt goes back as far as the written record. In fact, there are written records pertaining to debts that predate the invention of modern currency. In every culture, in every time, some human beings have found themselves unable to pay for the necessities of life, and because of this, they have borrowed money and goods to live. For the vast majority of history, when they could no longer pay back their debts, they paid with their labor, enslaving themselves or their children to their creditors. (Be grateful you were born in the modern era.)

Yet, even if debt has always been part of human society and will be for the foreseeable future, attitudes about debt changed over time. It doesn't take a rocket scientist to see that many common American beliefs about personal debt are not sustainable. Too many households continue to spend more than they bring in each month. If we continue to go deeper into debt, at some point we will not be able to make our payments, and it will have to stop.

In most times and places, people have used debt to pay for the necessities of life when they have no other means of doing so. However, many of us use debt to create a lifestyle that cannot be supported by our incomes over the long term. Such an obviously paradoxical way of thinking ought to cause us to laugh out loud at the irony. Consumer debt *always* makes the future worse than it could be because a chunk of your income must go to the debt service payments and interest. So eating out this month on the credit card makes eating out at all more difficult next month, and if there is a financial crisis, debt service payments can make it more difficult to pay for necessities like medicine or heat. In general, consumer debt should only be used for the most dire of emergencies.

One goal of this book is to help teach you new ways of thinking about debt. To do that, we will look at the effects of debt on our quality of life in detail. To begin, start by asking yourself: In what circumstances do you believe it is acceptable to go into debt? (Yes, this includes those credit cards you don't pay fully each month. Credit cards that are not 100% paid off at the end of the month are debt, period!) Each of us needs to examine the reasons we believe it is acceptable to use a credit card. If we want to change our financial situation for the better, each of us needs to understand the values that drive the choices we make each day. For now, don't try to change your behavior (unless you want to); just observe your thinking and spending habits. Look at the times you use a credit card. What kind of items do you buy on credit? Are they necessities? Are they impulse buys? Just spend some time observing yourself.

This isn't a right or wrong kind of quiz, so work hard to keep from judging your choices. Self-judgment acts as a trap that keeps many people from being able to change their ways. If you are going to adopt a new value system, you need to accept the one you have now and quit pretending someone else made all those financial decisions you regret. You might need to give yourself permission to be angry with yourself or cry. Don't worry about that; the rest of us are crying over our mistakes as well. You are not alone. Then, if you ever hope to change, you will need to forgive yourself and move on. Anger turned inward inhibits change like nothing else.

Ironically, many Americans believe they are alone in their financial woes. Yet my experiences as a financial counselor have shown me time and again, we are not alone in our suffering. I have counseled all levels of wealth, from those who live exclusively on social security, to C-list celebrities and those who live in Beverly Hills. The amounts of income may be different, but the stories are strikingly similar. Let's not forget that poor financial choices are not limited to individuals. Lehman Brothers, Bear Sterns, AIG, General Motors and Chevrolet didn't go under because they were financial geniuses. Governments are not immune either. The 2011 euro-zone crisis is simply a debt crisis on an international scale. The problem isn't yours alone, and it isn't just you who can't figure out a solution. Poor financial thinking is in the water. It is in the air that you and I breathe. It is part of our culture. So before you and I can find a new way to think, we will have to learn to recognize when our current culture gets in our way.

Why Fixing Our Country's Financial Problems Won't Be Easy

To understand just how deep our cultural problems with debt run, you need to know a little more about our recent economic history. I finally began to grasp just how dire our financial situation was as a country in the winter of 2009, when I heard a presentation by a Washington State University economics professor. He showed wages for all but the very wealthiest individuals in the United States had largely been flat since 1980, when adjusted for inflation. This means since 1980, for the average American, there has been no improvement in their financial well-being because any increase in wages was simply used up by rising prices for consumer goods. He pointed out our economy is approximately sixty-six percent to seventy percent driven by consumer spending. Then he simply asked a question: if consumers had no extra money to spend, how did our economy grow so nicely for twenty-eight years? It is no coincidence that credit card debt per person increased over ten times during the same period. Our total credit card debt as a nation peaked at just over $916 billion in 2008. For nearly thirty years, at least part of our economic growth rested upon a growing personal debt bubble. The overheated housing market of 2000 to 2005 was only the last spasm of this disease.

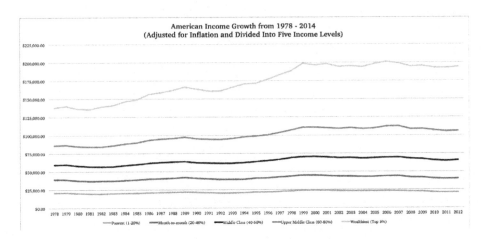

Data from the United States Census Bureau Historical Income Tables, Income Limits for each Fifth and the Top Five Percent

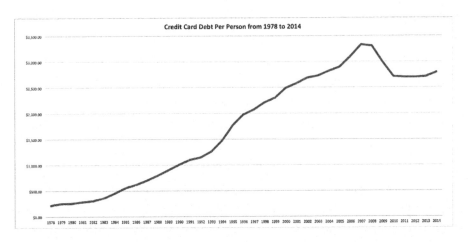

Data and Methodology: Federal Reserve Revolving Consumer Credit Owned and Securitized, Not Seasonally Adjusted December numbers divided by Census Bureau Annual and Monthly Population estimates from July from 1978 to 2014.

In 2007 and 2008 this thirty-year-old credit bubble collapsed and for a couple of years it looked like we might have learned our lesson. However, that hope quickly evaporated as personal debt started to rise as soon as the economy showed any signs of life. According to the Federal Reserve, at the end of 2014 credit card debt stands at just over $883 billion. The good news is that according to the National Foundation for Credit Counseling the percentage of families with a balance on their credit card has continued to drop, from 46 percent in 2007 to 38 percent in 2013. So while our overall consumer debt situation hasn't improved all that much, it does look like some families are learning to live without handing their financial well-being over to the credit card companies. The problem hasn't gone away; it's just concentrated in fewer families.

As people who have recently experienced the collapse of our credit bubble, this should sober us. It should make us think about what financial contingency plans we have made to protect our homes and our children from an economic storm that may come again. We may not know what the future of the economy will look like, and we may not know when we will feel like we are out of the woods, but good decisions on an ongoing basis can make the difference between weathering the storm with a few bruises and finding ourselves deeply in over our heads, facing dire consequences for the ones we love.

Americans used to take providing for their basic needs for granted. We didn't worry about food or shelter. How much has changed in such a short time. While the unemployment rate may have come down, our humbled economy no longer allows any of us to take our basic needs for granted. It is now possible to work very hard, to be employed full time, and still end up in a foreclosure, without adequate food, clothing, and transportation.

My Own Story

My career track record doesn't create the picture-perfect resume. Over the course of a decade I had too many different careers to make typical human-resource managers comfortable. However, not all of my changes in job and career were by choice. In 2004, I discovered real estate, and for the next four years I was happy in that profession. I built a good business as a residential real estate agent, but during those years the pickings were easy. Even though I made a better income than I had previously, I still struggled to get by. When you're starting out, real estate is either feast or famine.

Along the way, I made my share of financial mistakes. Once when money was tight, I refinanced my home, used the equity to pay off some debt and a car, and in the process raised my monthly mortgage payment nearly $400 per month—to this day, I deeply regret that decision. Even when times were good, we didn't seem to be able to get ahead. We lived from irregular paycheck to irregular paycheck. In between, we used a credit card or two to fill in the gaps. When the next paycheck would come, we would dump any extra onto the credit cards and put none of it in savings. What do you think would happen the next time a deal didn't close, and we had another gap? Out came the credit card.

In the winter of 2007, my parents invited my wife and me to take Dave Ramsey's thirteen-week *Financial Peace University* with them. What an eye opener! There were so many *"Aha!"* moments throughout the course of the seminar. We began building an emergency fund and applying Ramsey's baby steps to our personal finances. Ramsey's course provided key missing pieces that deeply influenced my thinking about money and saved my family from financial disaster. However, even while taking his course, I felt something didn't quite make sense. Ramsey's conspicuous consumption was continuously on display, and his plan still made becoming rich the end goal of healthy personal finance.

Reservations aside, Ramsey's classes helped, and none too soon. In the spring of 2007, the collapse of the real estate bubble began. By July, our finances dramatically tightened. Later that fall, there was a brief window during which I did pretty well by focusing on first-time buyers, but I could see what was happening. Ever since watching homes receive 30-plus offers in the summer of 2006, I had been worried about a bubble. As things ground to a halt in the fall of 2007, I figured the party was over. By early winter of 2008, the media had found their culprit. Do you remember those quaint arguments that said the majority of us were perfectly good borrowers, and it was just those evil sub-prime people who caused the problem? Denial is a deep river. By February, the handwriting was on the wall for many careers in real estate. In my area, there were nearly 1800 real estate agents and only 300 sales per month. I figured, if there were two sides to every transaction, my family would eat about one out of every three months. For some reason that wasn't good enough for me.

Late one night, I cried in my office as I decided to leave real estate. I really loved helping home buyers and home owners. Oh, if only I could have seen a bit farther the future! I quickly looked around for a profession that had a similar feel, and within a month, I landed a job as a financial adviser with AG Edwards. My first day was St. Patrick's Day 2008. Oops! I don't care how hard you work; it isn't the best decision to start a career as a financial adviser when you are staring at the biggest bear market since 1929. After two corporate mergers, I ended up working for Wells Fargo and washed out in May of 2010. In January of 2011, I took a job with a non-profit financial counseling agency to pay the mortgage. When that job ended in November, I finally gathered my thoughts and finished writing a book partially based on my experiences.

In America, we love winners. We love to talk about the person who made good against long odds. Dave Ramsey is a classic example. Ramsey has made a name for himself as a personal finance guru, because he has been a self-made millionaire twice, with a trip through the desert of bankruptcy in the middle. I think most of us figure that if the person has been able to dig out of bankruptcy and put together a million dollars, they probably know what they are talking about when it comes to personal finance. I think this is true, to a point. As I have already said, I personally benefited from Ramsey's thinking about debt. His class really saved me. I couldn't imagine what the last eight years would have been like without it. Now most of what seemed so strange then feels like second nature.

But we also like Ramsey's story because we like to think we will all become rich some day. We all hope we are the next multi-millionaire, and by all means; if you can get there, go for it. Nothing I say in this book will stand in your way. In fact it will help, and used well, wealth can truly help relieve the burdens of life. However, I want to let you in on a little secret: If we all became millionaires, then one hundred million or even one billion dollars would become the new standard of wealth. More importantly, milk would cost $300 a gallon. The scale of money would simply change, and it would still be the 1% vs. the 99%. Trying to become wealthy isn't the answer, and worse, acting like we are wealthy when we are not can deeply damage our financial stability for years to come.

Like Ramsey, I believe hard work is a necessary component to healthy finances, but the Ramsey story and other rags-to-riches tales have begun to ring hollow for me. I am more than a little tired of the fairy tale. After doing just what I was supposed to, where is my financial peace? What is the benefit of continuing to try when I haven't been able to get ahead? In some of my darkest moments, I have wondered why I shouldn't get a credit card and take my kids to Disneyland like my neighbors. From the fairy tale winners' corner there will always be the retort that I just haven't wanted it badly enough. I just didn't make enough dials while a financial adviser or knock on enough doors as a real estate agent. I admit to making my share of mistakes. Haven't we all, even the winners? But enough is enough! In our new economic reality many of us are going to do our best and still find ourselves making hard financial choices. Financial peace for the hard-working is no longer guaranteed. (Was it ever?)

The years following my decision to write *How to Manage Your Money When You Don't Have Any* have been paradoxically difficult, and inspiring. When I wrote the first edition of this book, I decided to go whole hog and continue on as a full time writer. It was a leap into the unknown, and I know this will sound crazy to some of you, but I believe I was called to that leap. I think I expected some kind of miracle. I would write a single book and all my financial problems would melt away. Yeah, well, not so much. We got by, just barely and we had help from others. There were moments of real darkness. Most of all, I deeply feared that I would fail as a provider for my children.

Not everyone greeted my decision to strike out as a full time writer positively. I had a few painful conversations, and some people chose not to take the journey with us. I used to say that the difference between me and a schizophrenic was that I knew I was having delusions of grandeur. Yet at the time I didn't see many options that would provide for my family. Things are stable now, but just barely, and only in the last year. Now, after sitting on step zero of my own financial plan for many years, we are finally beginning to move forward. No rags to riches story here. Let's call it rags-to-thrift store or a rags-to-Walmart story.

In truth, as hard as it was, I wouldn't change a thing.

My struggles have given me many gifts; one of which has been to make crystal clear to me that I love my three daughters and my wife tremendously. I would do anything to serve them. If I ever end up taking a below-living-wage job just to make ends meet, it will be primarily for their sake. Living through the difficulty of the last few years made me feel like a failure at times and, frankly, makes me distrust the financial fairy tale even more. I don't need the winners piling on with their insistence that the outcome would have been different if only I wanted it more. It doesn't help.

Yet, when I feel sorry for myself in the dark corners of the night, I find hope in this: I, unlike many of my neighbors, know what a tremendous difference it can make to keep your financial priorities straight, even when you don't have any money. By the grace of God, since 2007 we've managed to pay off all our consumer debt. We have preserved our home and we have food on the table. Despite years of declining income, only one pesky student loan and my home mortgage remain. When I first wrote this book, none of that was guaranteed.

At one point we found ourselves staring at a potential foreclosure. To tell the truth, even if I had lost my home, it might not have been so bad for my balance sheet. It wasn't what I wanted, but if it had happened, it wouldn't have been the end of the world, and it would have taken a huge debt burden off my shoulders. In the end, I didn't lose my home. It was refinanced into a forty-year mortgage, a choice I made only because it gave me the stability I needed to start moving forward.

I won... mostly. I have beat back my own personal financial crisis and found stability again, but I only won because I knew how to win, and because I consistently chose do the things it takes to win. Those choices made the difference between a frustrating but tolerable situation and an intolerable nightmare.

If you define financial success as having a million in the bank, I am not the writer for you. Go read the *Rich Dad, Poor Dad* guy. He will sell you the "secret" for becoming the next millionaire. (Good luck with that!) But if you define financial success as doing the best with what you have, then I have something to offer. It has been a rough ride in the last few years, but with experience comes wisdom.

Don't think this book relies on just my own wisdom either. As a real estate agent, financial adviser, and financial counselor, I've heard the stories of hundreds of different households. I counseled households from across the whole economic spectrum, and each household added its unique story to my financial thinking. Along the way, I learned that the poor can outshine the wealthy when it comes to financial wisdom. Theirs is the wisdom of scarcity. I have watched people from all income levels give up and fall into the cynicism of debt-based living. I've counseled single mothers who were one step away from losing the home that provided the last shreds of stability for their children. I grieved with them as they faced foreclosure and possible homelessness. If I have learned one thing from such stories, it is the power of choice. Keep choosing. Don't take the easy path. It makes a difference. Don't give in to the pressure.

Playing the Hand You Were Dealt

No one asks to be born into a generation that is not likely to do as well as their parents. However, for those of us who were born after the baby boomers it is a distinct possibility this will be our fate. I won't suggest we shouldn't be mad at the situation.

But, I believe acting on our anger never creates any useful change, and generations which followed haven't exactly avoided the excesses of our elders. Our own self-destructive financial choices make it unwise for us to throw stones.

In reality, it doesn't matter how we got to this point. The question is no longer how we avoid or get out of the trap laid for us by the rampant consumer debt of the last 35 years, but rather what we as individual households are going to do now that we are in this situation. Contrary to popular belief, there is a lot that can be done. We cannot change the hand we have been dealt, but we can play it to the best of our ability, which can make a tremendous difference in the outcome.

Mission, Strategy, and Tactics

When I was counseling struggling families, I found that most of us can't figure out how to think straight about money. We don't have any cultural handles that teach us healthy financial thinking. Most people seem wholly convinced that their FICO score is the best measure of their financial health. After searching hard, I ended up using the military planning model in my work as a financial counselor.

Military planning is useful for our financial thinking for several reasons. To start, it's useful because it takes apart the activities necessary to make changes breaks them down into useable chunks. It is designed to take an organization from the high level of setting goals all the way down to the individual activities that will support those goals. In my experience, that ability to work from goals to tangible activities gave hurting people a bright thread they could grasp to organize their efforts when things seemed darkest. It also helped that a military metaphor had the kind of crisis feeling these families needed.

Don't misunderstand, I'm not big on seeing everything in our culture as a battle or a war, but when you are just trying to keep your head above water financially, it feels like a battle, and acknowledging how hard families are working to stay on top of things can help them feel like someone understands. It also implicitly encourages individuals to take their finances seriously, something that we often don't do until we face a financial crisis. For all these reasons, we'll use the metaphor of military planning as the thread to hold together the different strands of this book.

Before we apply military planning to our own finances, we'll need to briefly look at how the military thinks about planning for a war.

In any military plan there are three different components. First, there is the mission set out by the Commander-in-Chief. This is the overall goal of the war. For instance, force the unconditional surrender of the Axis powers.

The mission is then delivered to the military, which has the task of carrying it out. Traditionally, the military breaks its planning into two tiers designed to accomplish a mission set by the President. The first tier of military planning would be the strategies the military chooses to complete the President's mission. In World War II the allies pursued a variety of strategies to defeat the Axis powers. Perhaps the most obvious strategy was the systematic liberation of almost all the territory held by the Axis.

The third component of traditional military planning is the tactics. These are the numerous day-to-day activities that achieve the military strategies used to accomplish the mission set by the President. For instance, the invasion of Normandy, D-Day, was a tactic used to accomplish the strategy of defeating Hitler's armies, which helped accomplish the Commander-in-Chief's mission to force the surrender of Germany.

So what happens when this system falls apart, when the enemy doesn't cooperate or when the mission isn't well thought out? When things start to go bad, military planners often replace clear strategic thinking with tactics. You see, tactics are the easiest piece for the military to control. It feels *good* to be doing something to make it right on the battlefield.

Many military historians accuse the United States of making this mistake during its participation in the Vietnam Conflict. You can watch an example of this mistake in the film *We Were Soldiers*. The movie portrays one of the first major American battles of the Vietnam War, the battle of Ia Drang. American troops won a hard-fought victory against a much larger Vietnamese force. However, the President hampered the ability of American military planners to make victories like Ia Drang stick, because while the President had set a clear mission—defeating the army of North Vietnam—he added all sorts of unclear and contradictory conditions, such as fighting the Vietnam conflict on the cheap and with only a few troops on the ground. The North Vietnamese Army also hampered American military planning, because they simply did not attempt to hold any territory. Rather, if the Americans showed up, they moved on and simply came back after the Americans left.

Faced with these difficulties, American military planners struggled to find strategies that allowed them to accomplish the President's mission. Since a clear and politically feasible strategy could not be found, planners tended to confuse tactics for strategies. In *We Were Soldiers*, placing infantry on helicopters became more than a tactic to deal with a highly mobile enemy. Instead, military thinkers exalted the helicopter to a strategy that could win the war and accomplish the President's goals. While tactics such as helicopter-based infantry won many short-term victories during Vietnam, these victories were never sustained and often quickly reversed, because American military planners lacked a credible strategic road map that allowed the tactics to work together toward a mission.

So why the military history lesson? Because many of us make the same kind of mistakes with our personal finances as our government did during the Vietnam conflict. We win many small victories, and even some major battles, but then wonder why it still feels like we are spinning our wheels. For instance, for a time we may manage to keep shuffling our credit card debt from one low-interest introductory offer to another. We may always pay all our bills on time and have a nearly perfect credit score. Yet we still feel we are falling further and further behind. Often, we have no problem finding tactics to win battles on a daily basis; instead, we lack a clear and reasonable financial mission and strategic plans to guide our daily financial choices toward that mission. To make sense of our financial situation, we need to take a step back from the day-to-day battles, look at where we are trying to go and what strategies we are using to try to accomplish these goals.

Your Financial

Mission

Chapter 2:
The American Dream

Westerners can easily forget that we live in an incredible time. The United States is still rightly called the land of opportunity. Each day, immigrants from around the world still arrive on our shores, because here they have the opportunity to make a better life for themselves and their children. Western nations provide their inhabitants with an ability to take care of daily needs beyond the wildest dreams of 99% of the human beings who have lived on this planet. We really shouldn't forget that. Even with our political and environmental concerns, this is a great time to be born. Sometimes in the middle of all the frustration, we just need to sit back, take a deep breath, and be thankful for what we have—and we have a lot. Despite our current economy, the American dream still seems very much alive for our new immigrants.

Yet, since our earliest days as a country, there seems to have been a split in the meaning of the American Dream. Just what did immigrants come to find on our shores? On the one hand, it seems to have embodied an idea expressed in the Norman Rockwell painting *Freedom From Want*.

In this famous painting we see a grandmother and grandfather bringing a turkey to a table surrounded by friends and family. All are smiling, including Rockwell himself, who looks out of the painting at the viewer from the bottom right hand corner. Rockwell's title uses the word "want" in the old-fashioned sense of the word, freedom from deprivation. All the basic needs of those in the painting have been met; they have no want.

This painting was part of a series of four paintings that Rockwell painted to sell war bonds during World War II. The series was titled *OURS... to Fight for*. If a modern reader can fault the painting for anything, it would be its lack of diversity. This is clearly a white, middle-class dream. That said, Rockwell captures well the dreams that have driven people of every ethnicity to our shores. In America we have a better opportunity to be free from want than in just about any other place in the world, and individuals and families have sought that dream for hundreds of years.

Yet, from the earliest days of our nation, this modest American dream has always competed with a more grandiose version. This grand American dream might be stated as freedom to have *everything* I want. One could easily fall into the trap of believing such thinking is only a post-World War II problem, but such is not the case. This definition can be seen in the land rushes and gold rushes of the nineteenth century as well as in the investment and get-rich-quick schemes of the twentieth. Pieces of it run through most contemporary books on personal finance, including Dave Ramsey's work, which emphasizes wealth creation as the end goal of all healthy personal financial thinking. Perhaps my very favorite expression of this grand American dream comes from the depression era song *Big Rock*

Candy Mountain, by Harry McClintock, which lays out a hobo's version of this grandiose dream.

If something has changed in the last seventy-five years, it has been that so many Americans currently believe this grand version of the American dream can be achieved. After World War II, our unprecedented wealth strongly tipped the balance in favor of the grand vision. For many in the western world, unprecedented prosperity allowed them to take finding adequate food, clothing, shelter, and transportation for granted. In the United States, Americans organized their lives around the pursuit of status, acceptance, and personal success.

None of this should be taken to imply that everyone has shared equally in our prosperity. During the twentieth century, many Americans, particularly those from racial and ethnic minorities, continued to struggle to meet their basic needs. However, during the post-war era, the voices of these groups had little representation in mainstream culture.

Unfortunately, the prevailance of the grand dream made the Great Recession all the more difficult for those who unexpectedly found themselves struggling to pay for basic necessities. Many formerly middle class households were unprepared to grapple with an economy that no longer guaranteed to meet the basic needs of all "hard-working" adults. The move backwards came as a shock.

Consider this chapter a chance to reshape your priorities. Let's begin by considering how our status-driven culture has reshaped our goals and thinking during the last seventy plus years. Along the way, we will look at a real-world example of how taking basic needs for granted leads to poor financial thinking, even among high income earners. Finally, we will consider what financial goals are reasonable in light of the lessons learned during the Great Recession.

Wants vs. Needs: An Opportunity for Business

When a person is concerned about their survival, they hold tightly to their resources, because tomorrow they might need them. It takes a lot for them to be convinced they have enough resources to spend them on a luxury item. Extra resources are much more likely to be saved for a rainy day. But what happens to our financial thinking if our concern about physical survival is taken away?

For an individual who is no longer concerned about their basic needs, a whole host of nebulous desires are now free to compete for that person's time and attention. Goods and services related to human needs can become undervalued, while those goods and services that provide perceived status, self-expression and prestige dominate a person's choices and financial thinking. In this system, wants have replaced needs as the primary concern in most financial planning.

However, these new desires are almost wholly matters of taste and opinion. The postwar dominance of taste and opinion in our culture's financial thinking created a whole host of new business opportunities. Luxury items and services designed to improve our quality of life took on a new importance. Since many of these items had little relationship to our survival companies had to find new ways to sell us their products. They encouraged a culture based on comparison, envy, and status in order to sell their wares. As we saw in the last chapter, this status based consumption has become the driving force behind our economy. Today consumer spending accounts for nearly 70 percent of our economic growth.

Because they depend on our continued spending on luxury items, many businesses, not to mention currently elected politicians, have a vested interest in making sure we do not begin to prioritize our basic necessities over continued consumer spending. After all, to take the necessities of life seriously again will come at a cost for all of us. Such behavior can damage our economy because it will slow consumer spending. This drop in consumer spending then feeds back on itself, causing more layoffs and worsening our economic situation. Thus many businesses and politicians would rather we didn't change our behavior, because it will make life more difficult for them.

However, a great many of us are buried under debt and lacking in savings. We really don't have much of a choice but to try to pay off our debt. The alternative is to continue forward down a very unproductive path of over-consumption and simply put off the day of reckoning for another few years. That may serve the interests of our currently elected officials and business leaders, but it is certainly not in your best interests, not until you have taken care of some other priorities first. Just keep that in mind the next time someone in business or government says that the answer to our problems is for the consumer to spend more. If you are struggling with basic necessities and have little or no savings, these "leaders" don't have your best interests at heart.

Since the end of the war, our country has created whole industries dedicated to persuading us to continue spending money on luxury items. The invention of the television just at the beginning of this wealth boom profoundly impacted the process by which advertisers accomplished their goals. More recently, the internet and social networking have opened avenues for marketing goods and services that couldn't have been imagined in the wildest dreams of the mad men of the 1960s advertising boom. Today, advertisers invest billions of dollars each year to discover what makes us choose to place our money with product X rather than product Y.

We could digress and talk about the thousands of different tactics advertisers use to convince us to purchase luxury products, but that won't help if we don't have our own priorities straight. Yes, every consumer should learn defense strategies such as looking at the bottom shelf in a grocery store and avoiding eye-level products, but other personal finance writers have written great books on marketing tactics.

For now, just keep in mind sellers need to make us *want* their products before their tactics will work. This is why in TV land, beer always gets you the sexy girl and why cotton fabric always appears at the most sentimental moments in our lives. Marketers work very hard to associate their products with the "good stuff" life offers. Then they leave it up to us to make the mistake of believing their product will provide the good life we want. The best defense against advertising is to make your own decisions about what you value and to maintain a skeptical attitude about the associations that advertisers try to make with their products. Since when is cotton more homey, sentimental and comforting than silk? Only since advertisers told us so. And since when does the consumption of beer lead to catching the sexy girl? If you're the one drinking, it may lead to sex—but not usually with the sexy girl, unless she's drunker than you are! If you know what you want out of life and you don't let advertisers trick you into believing their product will provide it, then advertisers have little control over what you purchase.

Before we turn to look at a set of financial priorities that trump both wants and status, I have one more thing to say regarding the relationship between consumers and business. Consumers must remember that every for-profit company in the United States has exactly the same goal: to make money for its owners. This includes the mom-and-pop restaurant down the street and the mega-bank with a branch in your local grocery store. Where do they get all that money for their owners? From you!

For these businesses, taking money from you and putting it in their pocket isn't a game; it's a matter of life and death. If they cannot extract enough money out of your pocket, they will go out of business.

Worse still, publicly traded corporations have the expressed goal of trying to *maximize* their profits for their stockholders. By necessity, this implies trying to take as much money out of your pocket as they possibly can. For many companies, especially national corporations, if they have to trick you through deceptive marketing or hidden fees, they won't hesitate to do so.

Every time a for-profit company interacts with you, their need for profit is their top priority. How could it be otherwise? Their survival depends upon it. They may sincerely believe customer satisfaction and quality products are important, but only as long as they help keep the company profitable.

I am not trying to keep you from shopping at your local supermarket or car dealer. I want you to patronize local businesses in your community. I am trying to remind you *no* seller cares about your financial well-being as much as you do. They care *most* about their own existence, and their continued existence depends upon taking money away from you. For business, *every* interaction with you is a deadly-serious struggle for your money all dressed up with a friendly smile and a thank you. How seriously do you take it?

Financial Freedom vs. Financial Stability

Let's take a quick second to sum up what I've argued so far. Until 2008, we lived in a culture dominated by a concern for luxury, status, and wants rather than basic necessities. However, for the majority of people, the pursuit of luxury has been a bit of an illusion for at least thirty years. Since 1980 the wages of most workers in the United States have been flat or even slightly in decline when you consider inflation. Our raises were simply eaten up by the growing cost of milk, gasoline, and car payments.

Instead, we worked harder. We worked more hours. The number of families in which both spouses worked outside the home grew significantly during that timeframe. When all of these weren't enough we borrowed money to make sure we could continue to buy our status and sense of well-being. The generations born after the Second World War grew up believing they could have *everything* they wanted, and when the economy didn't provide it, they borrowed to get it. Our recent economic and personal finance troubles are simply the inevitable hangover.

It's time we re-adopt a more modest vision of what wealth can provide us. While our land of opportunity is not capable of providing us with every consumer good and service we desire, it is still capable of providing us with unparalleled financial stability and freedom from real want. The pursuit of financial stability needs to replace the pursuit of financial freedom in our basic beliefs about what money can provide.

But what practical difference in our day-to-day living does it make if we pursue financial stability instead of wealth? So far, all of this has been a really great thinking exercise, but that is only one small step toward changing our daily lives and relieving the knots in our stomachs. An example provides the best way to see what a difference the pursuit of financial stability can make in our thinking.

Dentist vs. Receptionist

So what does it mean to be wealthy? Who is actually wealthy in the United States? Most of us believe wealth means having access to all the consumer goods and services we desire. Wealthy people are the people who have the most stuff. While that may be true, most people don't realize that access to stuff will not protect them from financial stress when difficult times arrive. Wealth is not equal to financial stability. To demonstrate my point, I want to give you an example I created for a seminar I taught at a low-income apartment complex. The salary numbers for the dentist are from the Bureau of Labor Statistics. It also comes from my experiences as a financial counselor. In my practice, both of these fictional characters were very typical.

We begin in the year 2005. The thirty-year credit boom is still on, and no one knows it is rapidly approaching its end. The housing market is red-hot, and the economy is still moving at a good clip, held up by our housing bubble. Let me introduce you to our two consumers.

Meet Dr. Bite:

Dr. Bite is a recently graduated dentist. By all our country's standards he has done quite well for himself. Three years ago he finished dental residency and was really quite lucky. Dr. Bite completed his residency with a local dentist who took a liking to him. This older dentist was looking to retire and hand his practice over to a younger dentist. Bill Bite was the perfect fit. Now, in 2005, he owns his own dental practice, which employs 5 other people.

He and his wife recently sold their first home in a not-so-nice neighborhood in Seattle proper. In the smoking hot housing market they did very well. They had ten offers in just over 24 hours, and the home sold for well above the asking price. This profit, plus Bill's income, allowed them to purchase a new home out of town with a beautiful view of both Puget Sound and the distant Olympic Mountains. Not only does their 3,600-square-foot home have a wet bar and small rec. room, but it also has its own media room complete with leather theater seating, and a sound system that can make your fillings vibrate. Bill Bite likes nothing more than to invite his buddies over on the weekends to watch the local Seahawks and Huskies. Each morning Betsy, who is a stay-at-home mom, drives their luxury SUV to a local private school to drop off their two children. Bill Bite is living the dream.

Introducing Samantha Smyle:

Sam works at the front desk in Dr. Bite's office. Her life has not turned out as she planned. Five years ago, right in the middle of her American dream, she was unexpectedly divorced by her creep of an ex-husband, who suddenly found one of his business colleagues more attractive. Her first year after divorce was incredibly difficult, but since then Sam has managed to find her footing. Two years ago she started taking classes at a local community college. She has been able to get a couple of grants and taken on a small amount of debt, but she mostly paid cash for her education. She plans to earn her Associates degree as well as a degree as a dental technician. She hopes that when she is finished, Dr. Bite will have a job for her. Since she needs to work full-time to pay for her schooling, she has only been able to take one or two classes at a time. She and her two children live in a decent apartment, which she recently rented not far from Dr. Bite's office. Her children are coping as well as can be expected. Her ex sometimes pays his child support, but the new girlfriend didn't work out so well, and since they split up he has been struggling to hold down a job. Sam suspects guilt is part of his problem, but she has never looked back. "One and done" is her motto. However, she cannot count his court-ordered child support in her budget. Anything she can get for the kids with that money counts as an extra. Most often, she puts it aside for a rainy day.

Now that we have met our characters, it is time to do something we almost never get to do, much to our detriment. Let's take a look under the hood, shall we? What does their financial situation really look like?

On the next couple of pages you will find side by side comparisons of each of their monthly incomes and expenses.

Monthly income and expenses 2005

Income

	Dr. Bite	Sam Smyle
Annual Income	$161,000.00	$31,000.00
Monthly Gross Income	$13,416.67	$2,583.33
Retirement	-$1,300.00	-$200.00
Health Insurance	$0.00	$0.00
Pre-Tax Income	$11,666.67	$2,383.33
Federal Tax Withholding	-$1,797.92	$0.00
Social Security	-$490.00	-$108.50
Medicare	-$169.17	-$37.46
Total Monthly Take-Home Pay	**$9,209.58**	**$2,237.33**

Expenses

	Dr. Bite	Sam Smyle
First Mortgage or Rent	$2,800.00	$850.00
Second Mortgage	$600.00	$0.00
Groceries, etc.	$800.00	$500.00
Car Insurance	$180.00	$65.00
Gasoline	$250.00	$110.00
Electricity	$120.00	$85.00
Natural Gas	$120.00	$0.00
Water / Sewer	$65.00	$0.00

Garbage	$65.00	$0.00
Cable TV / Internet	$150.00	$45.00
Cell Phones	$80.00	$80.00
Student Loan / College Tuition	$967.00	$100.00
Minimum Credit Card Payments	$432.00	$0.00
Car Payment 1	$415.00	$0.00
Car Payment 2	$512.00	$0.00
Private School Payments	$1,100.00	$0.00
Entertainment and Eating Out	$300.00	$50.00
Pocket Money	$150.00	$50.00
Emergency Savings	$0.00	$100.00
Savings for a New Car	$0.00	$200.00
Vacation Fund	$100.00	$0.00
Take Home Pay	$9,209.58	$2,237.33
Total Expenses	$9,206.00	$2,235.00
Total Left Over	$3.58	$2.33

Dr. Bite has everything. He drives a very nice car and so does his wife. He has an amazing home, and he has enough money to eat out and entertain his family. He even puts $100 away per month for an annual trip to Hawaii, the rest of which is financed by credit cards that he has no trouble paying. Most of us would look at Dr. Bite and say he is well off, perhaps not wealthy, but definitely upper middle class. We would think he has arrived.

On the other hand, Sam has just moved into the neighborhood that Dr. Bite left, and she is renting her apartment. She has little money left over each month and is able to take her small family out to eat only once a month and rarely to the movies. Most of us would say that she's in trouble financially because she is just struggling to make it by. Almost all of us would say that she is not as well off as Dr. Bite. She might even be called poor by some (ridiculous) standards. But what happens when you put each of these situations under stress? How do they play out? Let's jump forward five years and see how Dr. Bite and Sam are doing in 2010.

Dr. Bite in 2010

Let's drop in again on Dr. Bite and Sam in 2010. Things went along just fine for Dr. Bite until 2008, and then the last two years have been difficult. His business has been steadily declining since the beginning of the recession. Right now he is down about 25 percent from his peak in 2007. Recently, he made the mistake of looking through the records from the last thirty years of the practice he owns and found out there hadn't been a month as bad as last month since 1987. As the economy tanked in the last two years, it feels like all his clients have gone away. He swears that every other time the front desk calls to verify a six-month cleaning, they hear the same story. "I lost my dental insurance and can't afford it right now."

He has had to make some changes at work. To just keep the doors open he has taken a pay cut, so his pay is down 30 percent. Also, this year he finally decided he could no longer absorb the increasing cost of healthcare for his staff. Dr. Bite cares about his staff, and the meeting where he announced the changes ranks as one of the top ten worst moments of his life.

But there wasn't a choice; he just couldn't afford to continue to pay more. Since business is down, there is absolutely no more overtime, and he has asked a couple of his employees to cut back their hours to 35 hours per week. If something doesn't change he will have to lay someone off. Every time he thinks about it he feels sick.

Things aren't going so well at home either. It just feels like he and Betsy can't get ahead. They are still making their credit card payments, but just barely. There have been times where they have been late enough that they have had a call or two from the credit card companies. Not that all the juggling has really mattered: Bill and Betsy's credit card companies have still raised their interest rates to well over 20 percent. Now it feels like no matter what they do, they cannot make any headway at all.

So far, they have made every mortgage payment, but it has been a close thing and who knows what next year will bring. Secretly, he has considered selling their home, but when he talked to one of his Rotary buddies about it, the real estate agent didn't have encouraging words. The agent estimated that Bill and Betsy's home, which they purchased at $725,000, is only worth around $600,0000. Worse yet, Bill and Betsy used an 80/20 loan to purchase their home. That common loan product allows buyers to purchase a home without a down payment, using a second higher rate mortgage to pay the 20 percent of the loan not covered by a traditional mortgage. Bill found out from his friend that in Washington State, second mortgages become personal debt if they aren't paid off in the sale. After crunching all the numbers Bill figures that even if, he managed to sell, he would end up dragging around $50,000 in debt from a home that he no longer owns. When he asked his buddy what he should do about his second mortgage, he suggested bankruptcy.

It really doesn't feel like much of an option to sell, but it is slowly dawning on Dr. Bite that he may have no choice.

Thank goodness one of the cars has been paid off. That helped the budget significantly, but Betsy keeps pressuring him to get a new one. She says she doesn't feel safe in a six-year-old vehicle. She kept warning him that her car was going to break down, and sure enough it did. Thank goodness it happened at home, and the fix was relatively cheap, but now Betsy won't let go of the idea that her car is unreliable. Now she keeps telling him she is going to break down on the freeway one day, and she and the children will be left stranded. The image of his kids stuck in a car on I-405 keeps rattling around in his head, and that has kept him up at night.

Sam Smyle in 2010

The last couple of years have not been easy for Sam Smyle either. Prices for everything keep going up, but she hasn't seen a raise since 2005. That said, she seems to be weathering the Great Recession better than some. Her boss, Dr. Bite, has been having an especially hard time. He has always run his business like a family. When he told his staff they were going to have to pay for part of their healthcare this year, he had tears in his eyes. The thing is, after her ex, Greg, left, Sam has never taken her financial situation for granted again. She has always made sure there is something extra each month. Sam just rolled with the change in expenses. Eating out has all but gone away, and going to the movies is a thing of the past. So is the daily latte habit. Instead, Sam and the dental assistants went in together and bought an espresso maker for the office. They make their own lattes now. One of the assistants used to be a barista, so they don't come out half bad. Those changes alone made a huge difference and were no-brainers for Sam.

A layoff doesn't seem as far-fetched to Sam as it did even a few months ago. Dr. Bite asked two of the younger members of his staff to cut their hours. If things don't turn around soon at the practice, there will have to be more cuts. There has been talk among the other assistants they could even end up job sharing, that is, working part time and taking unemployment part time. That really got Sam thinking about whether or not she could handle a layoff. Knowing she has savings in the bank has allowed her to sleep at night, but if she lost her job, she realized she would probably have to get a roommate. Frankly, once she considered the idea, she decided she might just pursue it to keep up her savings. She couldn't count the number of times in the last few years her emergency fund has really saved her. From paying for stitches, to the month in which she was so tired she forgot to include the electric bill in the budget, her savings has kept her afloat.

If a layoff happened, one possible option might be to quit school, but she only has two semesters left, so that is probably the last thing she would consider. With her emergency fund, she would have the cash to pay for those classes outright, but if she lost her job she would need that cash to pay for basic necessities like food. So far, Sam has avoided most student loans, but considering how close she is to finishing, she might consider reducing the amount of her tuition she pays in cash and borrowing for the rest. It wouldn't be that much debt, and since she does payroll in the office, she knows just how much better money a new dental assistant makes than she does.

She can't say she's happy about her current financial situation, but she really is better off than some. In the office the other day she overheard a tense conversation between one of the other assistants and her husband. They are so upside down in credit card debt, they are going to have to look seriously at bankruptcy or drop their health coverage. Sam is just grateful she paid off all her credit card debt with some of the money she received in the divorce. She doesn't think she could sleep at night if she also had credit card debt to think about. By the looks of the dark circles under her coworker's eyes, it looks like she isn't sleeping well.

Monthly Income and Expenses 2010

Income

	Dr. Bite	Sam Smyle
Annual Income	$112,700.00	$31,000.00
Monthly Gross Income	$9,391.00	$2,583.33
Retirement	-$930.00	$0.00
Health Insurance	-$650.00	-$380.00
Pre-Tax Income	$7,811.00	$2,203.33
Federal Tax Withholding	-$834.00	$0.00
Social Security	-$328.06	-$108.50
Medicare	-$113.26	-$37.46
Total Monthly Take-Home Pay	**$6,535.68**	**$2,057.37**

Expenses

	Dr. Bite	Sam Smyle
First Mortgage or Rent	$2,800.00	$850.00
Second Mortgage	$600.00	$0.00
Groceries etc.	$1000.00	$650.00
Car Insurance	$220.00	$85.00
Gasoline	$450.00	$200.00
Electricity	$120.00	$85.00
Natural Gas	$120.00	$0.00

Water / Sewer	$85.00	$0.00
Garbage	$85.00	$0.00
Cable TV / Internet	$220.00	$0.00
Cell Phones	$150.00	$30.00
Student Loan / College Tuition	$967.00	$100.00
Minimum Credit Card Payments	$612.00	$0.00
Car Payment 1	$425.00	$0.00
Car Payment 2	$0.00	$0.00
Private School Payments	$1,500.00	$0.00
Entertainment and Eating Out	$300.00	$00.00
Pocket Money	$250.00	$00.00
Emergency Savings	$0.00	$50.00
Savings for a New Car	$0.00	$00.00
Vacation Fund	$100.00	$0.00
Take Home Pay	$6,535.68	$2,057.37
Total Expenses	$10,004.00	$2,050.00
Total Left Over	-$3,468.32	$7.37

If Dr. Bite came into my financial counseling office, my news for him would feel grim. He does have financial options that could make his situation better, but I doubt he would accept any of them, because every one of them would dramatically change his lifestyle. Dr. Bite is living his life trying to satisfy all his material wants. The high amount of self-worth and value he receives from material goods will not make it easy for him to recognize he can no longer afford his current lifestyle. He certainly cannot afford to purchase a new car for his wife. More importantly, unless he finds a way to reduce his monthly expenses, he is likely to end up in bankruptcy in the very near future. There are many options available to Dr. Bite, but in our culture of "financial freedom" and having everything you want, he is in a much deeper financial bind than Sam.

Think about that for a minute! Dr. Bite started out making five times as much as Sam. Even after taking a significant reduction in income, he still makes four times her income. Yet, it is the supposedly well-off person who faces bankruptcy. Have you ever wondered how billionaires can end up going bankrupt? How is it so many sports superstars make millions and millions while playing sports and then go bankrupt in only a few years? This is how they do it. They take their eye off the ball, take their basic needs for granted, and end up with no way out when the inevitable financial stress comes.

As much as we assure ourselves we would never behave that way if we ever "made it," many of us are just like Dr. Bite. Every time you stand in line for the newest Apple product without putting money aside for emergencies, you are pursuing the wrong American dream. Every time you use credit to pay for something, knowing full well that you will pay interest on it, you are risking your financial future and condemning yourself to a lifestyle that is worse than what your paycheck could provide. As a nation, we can no longer afford to let the pursuit of "financial freedom" get in the way of the pursuit of financial stability. Our pursuit of the wrong financial goals takes away our options and leaves us vulnerable to downturns like our current one, and it hurts our families.

So what are those obstacles that keep us from taking care of our financial stability first? What holds us back from pursuing financial stability, and what can we do about it, other than paying a therapist for the next three years? These will be our topics in the next chapter.

Chapter 3:
Morality and Money

How you spend your money reflects your true values. Stop and think about that for half a second. I mean it more literally than it may sound at first. It isn't a metaphor. Unless you are a trust-fund baby, the money you have to spend on a monthly basis represents your hard work. Imagine for a moment that you are holding all the money you earned last month in cash. Unless you have savings, that cash is all your potential buying power for the month. Credit allows you to spend next month's work early. However, using credit now means you will have less money to spend next month, because next month, some of your income will have to go to pay off the extra money you spent this month. When you use debt you trap yourself in a cycle of ever-diminishing freedom.

So as you hold your money in your hand, imagine in front of you all the things that money could buy for you. Even if your paycheck is small, it is a world of almost infinite possibility. The problem is, your money is not infinite. Your money has infinite potential as long as it is in your hand, but that potential is immediately lost when you actually buy something. The potential has been used up. Now you have less money in your hand and you have the thing you purchased. The fact that our money runs out forces us to make choices about where we spend our money. When we make those choices, we are explicitly demonstrating that we value the things we chose to purchase over all the other goods and services we chose to avoid. How we spend our money reflects our true values at that moment in time.

No one forces you to spend your money on any particular item. Your money doesn't tell you where it needs to be spent; your values do. If you value food, you will spend some of your money on food. If you value what your spouse says and spend your money in the way they want it spent, you are choosing to invest in their respect and acceptance. When you purchase the latest video game—leaving yourself with little money to pay for food and only a partial rent payment—you are showing that you value a video game more than you value food and shelter. When you purchase that game on credit, because you do not have enough money to purchase it for cash, you demonstrate that you value a video game more than next month's food and rent.

Why We Don't Look at Our Bills: Emotions and Values in Conflict

Many of us find ourselves emotionally conflicted because the goods and services we actually buy don't match up with what we wish we valued, or what we say we value. Worse yet, values change, sometimes very quickly. What we valued in the moment may not be what we later wish we had valued. When we see this kind of behavior in ourselves, it creates all sorts of emotional conflicts and internal stress. Now, morality and ethics are all mixed up with our money.

We feel badly because we are embarrassed that we got a new iPhone despite telling our daughter she couldn't play soccer this fall because, "we couldn't afford it, honey." On top of the actual stress of managing all those bills, we add a heaping helping of shame and guilt. Is it any wonder that many of us have developed a large and unhealthy toolkit of avoidance behaviors and coping mechanisms? Some of us even take out our credit cards and spend money to assuage our guilt for overspending. Yikes! "How's that working for you?" says the Dr. Phil cherub on our shoulder.

There really isn't any easy way around it. For most of us, finding a way forward financially will mean facing the bad feelings and pain we have been putting off. We need our own day of reckoning. Many of us are already in the middle of that day. The economy brought it to us, ready or not. If you're reading this book, I bet you already recognize that you can no longer ignore the pain. The question is, what can we do about it?

Learning to Accept Yourself

Whenever I sit down to work with a family or an individual on their financial situation, I start by telling them there are no right or wrong answers to any of my questions. I want them to understand that they are not going to be scolded for their choices. Some financial counselors love to spend their time trying to make the finances of their clients look just like their own. While it may make the counselor feel superior to the client, it probably won't help the client. Of course, I point out areas where I think my clients could make changes that would help them, but in the end, their values determine which changes they will make.

"But wait a second!" I can hear you say, "Didn't you just spend the last two and a half chapters telling us we shouldn't value status items over our basic necessities? Isn't that telling us what to value?" You are perfectly correct. Throughout this book, I make the assumption that you value items like food, clothing, and shelter more than you value luxury items like new video games, a new iPhone, or a vacation to Hawaii. We all make mistakes, and sometimes we value status items more than necessities. Hopefully, these are not the majority of our moments and hopefully we seek to change and improve so these mistakes don't threaten our financial stability.

However, I could be wrong, at least some of the time. There have been clients who have surprised me. I once met a recently divorced woman with no children who owned a horse. As we examined her budget, it became very clear she was in danger of losing her home. She needed to make a decision between her home and her horse. Even if she did give up her home, it would still be difficult for her to find adequate shelter without giving up her horse. After I explained the situation, without even blinking an eye, she looked at me and said, "I will keep the horse." That isn't the answer I would give, but I am not a horse person, and who am I to tell her she is making the wrong decision? If she is willing to be homeless to keep her horse, am I to tell her otherwise? I hope the back seat of her car is a comfortable place to sleep. My job as a financial counselor was not to try to convince her to give up her horse. Rather, my job was only to show her the choice she must make between a decent place to live and her horse. Her values are her own choice.

Often, I find a large amount of our inner conflict about finances comes from our unwillingness to really look at what we truly value, and stand by it with integrity. We allow perception, the opinions of others, or perhaps religion to tell us what we should value, rather than owning up to what we truly value. Many of us have had our brains so addled by the continuous bombardment of advertisers, we don't even know what we value. An early step in taking control of our financial situation must be a kind of radical honesty and acceptance when it comes to our actual values. Only this kind of honesty and acceptance will allow us to seek clearly the changes we need to make in our value system.

Sometimes values and finances become a bit like a Chinese finger puzzle. Our desired values say one thing, and our financial choices say another. We find ourselves pulling as hard as we can to get out of the trap. We keep making purchases that another piece of us wishes we didn't make. It doesn't work, and we usually serve up lots of shame and guilt along the way. For myself, I find I need to respect my values as they are. This doesn't mean I give up on my desire to change them. On the contrary, I find that acceptance is the first step toward change. When I reserve judgment on my actions, I am often much more able to understand what motivates my behavior, and this lets me move forward. When we refrain from judgment, it is like we have stopped our efforts to pull against the Chinese finger trap. Once we stop, we can relax and find a way out of our dilemma.

At times, I can be frustrated with the outcome of a choice I made and tempted to be angry with myself. I find that I am my own harshest critic. However, when I take a few minutes, reserve judgment, and instead just think through why I made the choices I made, no matter how painful the reason, I sometimes find there is more merit in my decisions than I give myself credit for. No matter what the outcome, by putting off my self-criticism and paying attention to my choices, I find myself in a much better position to understand my values and change them in the future.

Once we have a true handle on what we really value, those areas where our actual financial values don't match up with our desired financial values will quickly become evident. It may also become quite clear that our financial values differ from those around us, perhaps with those we care about most, such as our spouse and family. That is the next topic we will explore.

Money in Relationships

There are as many different ways to manage money in relationships as there are different kinds of relationships. That is one of the things I enjoy most about being able to sit down with families and look over their finances. Every relationship is somewhat like a fingerprint, and the way each couple manages money reflects their unique point of view on the world. I am not here to tell you how to manage money with your partner. That is for the two of you to negotiate. I have met successful couples who do not have joint finances. They have an amicable agreement about who is taking care of what necessities. However, most couples adopt some sort of joint finances, and in these situations, there are some basic principles that tend to make managing money much easier.

First, managing the family finances usually runs more smoothly when it is everyone's job. One of the classic mistakes made in managing money in marriages is to assign the job of money management to one partner or the other and leave the kids out altogether. This creates all sorts of dangers and traps that can be difficult to avoid. First, only one person's values are incorporated into the financial plan, or at least one person's values are usually highly favored. This often leads to resentment by the other spouse.

When one person manages the money, the money manager tends to act as a parent, and the non-manager tends to act like a child. The parent is put in the position of saying "no" to the desires of the child, and the child acts resentfully toward the parent. This isn't exactly a recipe for relationship bliss.

I would argue, even if one person tends to manage the finances, all important financial decisions should be made by mutual agreement. This may make for some long and difficult conversations, but when both parties agree on what is to be done with the money, it helps keep resentment from building up in the relationship, and it keeps one partner from acting out in ways that undermine a family's ability to take care of their basic necessities.

There is another reason to keep the family finances a project for both partners. I actually wouldn't mention it, but I have seen it too often in my counseling practice to avoid it. If one person acts as the financial manager and they make a mistake, sometimes they will hide that mistake from their significant other. It may not be an obvious mistake. They may simply not understand until very late in the game that their strategies for managing the family money cannot work. They will often try to fix the problem without letting their partner know what has happened. This problem can be easily avoided if both partners give their input into each financial decision. That way if the couple makes a major blunder, no partner is alone in taking the blame. In this way the family sinks or swims together.

Next, the vast majority of conflict can be avoided if both partners' values are treated with equal respect. Think of this as extending the acceptance and grace we talked about in the last section to your spouse. I may have absolutely no interest in seeing our family money spent on new electronics, or new furniture. I may want it put toward a better family vacation, and I may feel taken for granted by my spouse. However, it will not help if I begin to judge them for their choices. As soon as I pass judgment, I will end up right back in the Chinese finger trap we discussed in the last section, because my spouse will most likely resist my efforts to shame them into doing what I want. If they don't openly resist, they will likely make their disapproval known somewhere else along the way. Acceptance and an attempt to understand go a long way to keeping tough negotiations calm.

If you believe your partner threatens the financial stability of the relationship with their spending, you will need to calmly ask them to examine their priorities. Then listen as they explain how they would accomplish their goal while protecting the safety of your household. You do not have to agree, and the most difficult financial negotiations happen here. If the two of you cannot agree, someone will have to compromise. For what it is worth, as long as both parties have negotiated in good faith, I believe it would be better to err on the side of caution when it comes to a family's financial stability.

Disagreements may also arise because of a difference in priority when it comes to the money left over after basic necessities have been met. In the end, these decisions may come down to a serious horse trade or two to find a means by which both spouses can agree. For instance, if my partner wants to purchase a new iPad or another electronic gadget, I may ask for the same amount of money to go into the vacation fund, and that the planned trip to the Grand Canyon be extended by one day. Finding solutions that both parties see as equitable can be hard work, but it will really go a long way to both improving your relationship and keeping your family on track financially.

In conclusion, it is much easier to manage a family's finances when both parties have adopted the same overall mission. To go back to the metaphor from the first chapter, it is very difficult to organize the strategies and tactics if the leaders cannot agree on what war they are to fight and what they want to accomplish. Helping partners adopt common financial goals is one of the reasons I am writing this book. My wife has noted that before we got our financial priorities straight, we fought often, and our fights were almost never directly about money. Yet, after we got on the same page, 80% of our fights disappeared. Hard work here is worth your effort.

Banks, Government, and Other Morality Police

Before we move on from the topic of values, morality, and money, there is one other set of actors I need to mention. I have argued morality and money get all tangled up because the choices we make with our money comprise one of the truest measures of our actual values, and conflict often arises when we wish we valued something different. To begin to change the way we spend our money we need to recognize and accept our current values system and how we use our money to support that value system. Once we accept our current system, it becomes much easier to change it and adopt a more useful set of priorities.

It is worth taking a moment to remember there are those who do not want us to get our financial priorities straight, because it doesn't serve their interests. In the last chapter I pointed out how a company's existence depends upon removing enough money from your pocket to keep themselves profitable. If they cannot accomplish this goal they will cease to exist. Worse yet, publicly traded corporations have the express goal of maximizing the profit they make from you to give that profit to their stockholders. Companies will not hesitate to use shame, fear, and even morality to convince you to purchase their product.

The company OnStar, sells a product, that among other things, allows you to contact 911 in your car with the push of a button. For several years they used to put out ads featuring actual 911 calls from traumatized children rescuing their parents after an emergency. As a dad, I always want my children to be able to get help in an emergency. Don't I have a moral and ethical duty to purchase OnStar for them? Aren't I a failure unless I protect them with this necessary product? Nonsense, but very emotionally effective! The effect is all the more jarring because I am usually listening to my radio to relax while driving, and suddenly my vehicle is invaded by a traumatized child and an earnest 911 operator. I cannot say I haven't had an adrenaline rush listening to these actual calls. Frankly, I find that kind of marketing offensive, and being a bit of a rebel, I decided I would never purchase OnStar until they quit interrupting my drive with an unwanted rush of fear. (Due in no part to my rebellion, they have since changed their marketing campaign.)

Your bank has no scruples regarding how they play on your emotions and sense of duty, either. Their obligation is to their stockholders, not to your wallet, and their main product is debt, a product that is rarely good for your financial health. Banks are not your friend, and in the run up to the collapse they stooped pretty low to convince you to keep purchasing their product.

Banks try numerous methods to keep you from changing your value system and financial goals. This isn't the time to go into all of them. I think you will begin to see them when you understand how high the stakes are for the bank. However, two different tactics are worth mentioning in the context of a conversation regarding values and morality, because they are such explicit attempts by financial institutions, companies, and the government to keep you from adopting healthy financial goals.

At the risk of offending some readers, I am going to make my point bluntly and then take some time to unravel the threads. Just do me a favor and practice that skill of reserving judgment before you slam the book closed in disgust. Here goes: no individual has a *moral* obligation to pay any of their bills. Now please don't misunderstand, I think you have all sorts of good reasons to pay your bills including your own integrity. Let me be clear; I want you to continue to pay your mortgage if you can, as long as your mortgage serves the best interests of your family. However, the moment that mortgage interferes with your duties to your partner or your children, you have a much higher obligation to put their interests above those of the bank. This may mean that you choose to stop paying your mortgage and allow your home to be taken by the bank, which is their right.

Especially during the housing crisis, I heard commentator after commentator decry the evils of those who no longer paid their mortgages. Some of them, even some of the smarter consumer financial experts, have argued homeowners have a moral obligation to pay. I vehemently disagree with this point of view.

Perhaps the easiest way to understand why I have no moral obligation to pay is to ask the question whether or not my bank feels a *moral* obligation to me. What will happen if through no fault of my own, I am no longer able to pay my mortgage? If I am not able to find work in the next few months, will my bank feel any moral obligation to me when six months go by and it is time to foreclose? Will they feel any obligation to keep my children from becoming homeless at the expense of their stockholders? Absolutely not! Nor should they! They have a duty to their stockholders, and I have a duty to my children. They will make a business decision based on profit and the stipulations of the contract I signed. They will point out to me: I have violated the contract, and they will take the action that the laws of the state allow them to take. They will take away my home, and if I have not made other arrangements, they will leave me homeless. That is their right under the contract I signed and the laws of Washington, my home state. So if the bank feels no moral obligation to me when I fall on hard times, why am I morally obligated to them? Why am I obligated in some way to accept such an asymmetrical relationship? In addiction circles I believe this is called a co-dependent relationship.

It's such an important point and it runs contrary to so much we are taught in our culture that it's worth repeating. If the bank feels no moral obligation to me but rather only a contractual obligation, then I have no moral obligation to them either. I have a contractual obligation to the bank. That contract states the consequences for me if I break it, and the bank is free to execute the consequences accordingly, but I have no obligation to them beyond that contract. I do, however, have a deep moral and ethical obligation to my partner and my children. If paying my mortgage is no longer in their best interest, then I have a duty to stop paying my mortgage and accept the consequences.

The attempt to morally obligate me to the bank is such an obvious fallacy, it is a sign of how far we have been drawn into the tactics of corporate bank marketing that we don't immediately begin to laugh when someone repeats the lie. Perhaps it is because so many men and women in suits sat on CNBC during the crisis and fulminated about evil homeowners that we were taken in. They all looked like they knew what they were talking about.

The second area where banks have been very successful in convincing us to morally obligate ourselves to them has been through the credit score system. I cannot tell you how many clients walk into my office and tell me proudly, they have never been late on a payment to their credit card company. Then I look at their monthly expenses and find, while they have never been late to the credit card company, they have no emergency fund, skimp on food, and cannot repair their car. Yet huge amounts of their value and worth seem to be invested in the fact they have made their payments on time. Ridiculous! Let's take that seriously for a second. If the goods and services you purchase with your money are a true reflection of your values, then a person who pays their credit card before feeding themselves has been so hijacked by bank marketing and scare tactics they actually value the bank's interests more than their own health and that of their family.

This kind of thinking needs to stop. Please do not misunderstand; I believe strongly in personal integrity, and paying your bills is almost always in the best interests of your family, so you should do so on time. Besides, when I give my word to someone, I need to follow through on what I said for my own sense of self-respect. I should be embarrassed if I cannot keep my word. However, when I use a credit card or when I borrow money from a bank, I have not given them my unconditional word. I have signed a contract. The contract and the law stipulate the limited consequences if I do not follow through with my end of the bargain. (These enlightened limits keep me from having to sell my children into slavery if I cannot pay.) On the other hand, I believe that I do have a nearly unlimited ethical and moral responsibility to myself and my family. If my debts are causing me to no longer meet my moral and ethical duty to my family, I have no moral obligation whatsoever to my bank. That thinking is a lie that serves the interests of the bank at the expense of children and families. It is wrong! (The congregation may now rise and turn with me to page 35 in their hymnal where we will sing....)

I hope this chapter demonstrates the need for a kind of radical honesty with ourselves when it comes to our financial choices. For some of us, it becomes painful to look at the money we wasted in the past when we currently face such financial insecurity. It can also be painful to try to negotiate with spouses and others regarding financial matters. However, in the end, such hard work is worth it if we can re-prioritize our spending and put our family's financial stability above our desires for financial freedom. If we can agree to keep our financial stability foremost in our financial choices, we cat take steps to change our status driven culture and to increase the sense of prosperity and security we all desire.

Your Financial Mission:
To secure your basic needs both now and in the future, and to do nothing that would harm your ability to secure them on an ongoing basis

Back during the Great Recession I had lunch at which I reminisced about the "good old days" with a gentleman. Before the collapse, he had had a pretty good sales career, making a six-figure salary. He had been accustomed to ordering suits and shirts with monogrammed cuffs. Now, he figured, his monthly budget would be workable if he brought in around $3,000 a month. It wasn't a lament. What amazed my lunch partner was how his tastes and definitions of needs had changed. Both of us marveled at how much less complicated our lives had become when we removed the pursuit of status and wealth from our financial thinking.

Is it any wonder that concerns about status and wants lead to poor financial thinking? Human desire is an unlimited and boundless ocean, a body of water that can never be filled. If we make our wants and our desires for status into our financial mission, then we are doomed to fail from the start, because just as we think we have made it, there is always another hill to climb. When asked how much money was enough, John D. Rockefeller is said to have replied, "Just a little bit more." Satisfying all of our material wants and desires is not an achievable financial goal even for the wealthy, let alone for us mere mortals. If our country is going to develop a healthier financial and economic mission, such financial goals are best abandoned.

However, achieving a kind of financial stability that allows us to sleep at night through all but the most disastrous of economic hurricanes can be achieved. Such a route may never provide us with a second home at the beach, but living by this goal, we can make sure that we do our best with what life brings. The funny thing is, when we make financial stability our goal, most of us find that we are more satisfied with our lives. Many of us will also be able to sleep at night for the first time in a long time. Considering all the tricks and traps we use to avoid the truth of our financial situation, our unconscious mind may have a better handle on reality than we do. It keeps waking us up, telling us to change course. Whether we understand it or not, freedom from want is back as the American dream.

Strategies

Chapter 4:
Is Your Boat Sinking?

In the previous section, we looked at how we as a nation tend to set goals for our personal finances, goals that have caused huge problems for our society. We saw how our current culture puts its efforts into purchasing luxury and status items because until 2008 our society ably met the basic needs of a large majority of its hard-working citizens. I argued this culture of perceived status and luxury has made it very difficult for many of us to recognize that our current economy no longer guarantees the basic needs of hard-working people. I believe it is time for us to re-adopt a simpler and healthier American dream, a dream in which we seek financial stability rather than wealth creation. But what does financial stability look like? How do we measure it? This chapter is meant to give you a start on answering those questions for yourself.

Is Your Boat Sinking?

To begin thinking strategically about your personal finances, I want you to ask yourself: on a month-to-month basis am I able to pay all of my bills without using credit? I am always surprised at how many people think it is normal to use credit to purchase the basic necessities of life. I often use the metaphor of a boat to help them understand their situation. Think of your household finances as a boat. If on a month-to-month basis you are able to pay all of your bills then your boat is water-tight. It is not leaking.

However, if you are deeply in debt and on a month-to-month basis you use credit cards or some other means to get by, you have two problems. Most people came to my financial counseling office for the most obvious but least worrisome problem: their financial boat was full of debt. Often these people were just inches from sinking when they walked in the door to ask for advice as a last-ditch effort to avoid the bankruptcy attorney down the hall. They believed their current debt payments were their primary problem

However, as I looked at their financial situation, I found for many of these folks they had a second much more serious problem. In many cases, their expenses on a month-to-month basis were significantly greater than their income. Their financial boat had a great big hole in it, and they were only worried about emptying out the boat. As I explained to these clients, they could go ahead and file a Chapter 7 bankruptcy and clear out the boat, but if on a month-to-month basis they did not make any changes, they would soon be right back in the same position. Next time they would not have the option of clearing out the boat with a bankruptcy, because Congress has caught on to that little scheme and now only allows a borrower a single Chapter 7 bankruptcy every eight years. Eventually, when their boat is full of water again and they cannot pay their bills, their creditors would begin garnishing their wages to pay back their debt. When the garnishments start, it would become 25% harder to make ends meet.

So I ask you, on a month-to-month basis, can you get by without borrowing money? Do you have enough income to meet all of your needs? Some of you will instantly know the answer is no. You already understand changes are necessary, either income must come up or expenses must go down. Your boat has a leak, and no matter what else you do to solve the problem, you need to fix that leak or your boat will sink. Hang in there. There is a way forward even if you cannot see it yet.

Some readers will confidently answer yes, and some of them will be right. But are you sure? Have you ever really added it up, or are you just saying that because there is always money in your checking account? At the beginning of a downward debt spiral there is always money in the checking account because the debt service payments are not yet big enough to be a problem. Yet when you add up your expenses and include those items you purchase on credit every month, you may very well have expenses that outstrip your income. So again I ask, do you really *know* whether or not you are making it on a month-to-month basis? Some of you will be shocked to find out the answer is no.

Still another more interesting group will answer, "I don't know." This is the group that needs to spend some heart-to-heart with their bank statements and credit card bills. At least you are honest about your denial. You have that going for you. That is better than the people who say, "Yes" but have never really looked at it. However, any kind of progress you hope to make toward financial stability requires you to know exactly where you are financially at all times. For those of us who are facing real financial hardship, accurate knowledge of our weak financial situation can be very frightening. Believe me, I personally understand. I spent three years terrified because I never knew if I was going to make the next mortgage payment. But if I was going to make good decisions about where I put my scarce dollars, then I had better know exactly what kind of dangers I faced.

Don't worry, I won't leave you high and dry. In the tactical section of the book we will deal with practical and simple ways to know exactly how much money you have at any moment in time, and they don't include writing down all your expenses every month. Right now, all I want is for each group to recognize that finding financial stability is impossible if you have a monthly budget that requires you to borrow money to live. It just won't work. To accomplish our goal of financial stability, one of our strategic plans must be to live without using debt for regular monthly expenses, except in extreme emergencies.

So What Are Necessities Anyway?

Our culture of status and luxury has warped the meaning of the word "need" like no other. All of us, not just our children, are prone to see our needs in overly broad terms. For those of us trying to adopt financial strategies that lead toward financial stability, it is a worthwhile exercise to consider just what goods and services we should prioritize with our limited resources.

To avoid all the excesses of the word "need," let's step out of our financial thinking for a moment and start with a bit of a blank slate, shall we? What must human beings have to continue to live? Proper food and water, clothing, shelter, and air come to mind. So far the last one remains free. (Although I am sure that if your local government could find a way to tax the oxygen you use, they would.) However, human beings must work to acquire each of the other three basic needs: food, clothing, and shelter. In fact, almost all human effort since the dawn of our species has been spent to support these three needs.

Take a moment and see again the picture I presented earlier. You are standing with your last month's pay in hand, looking out over all the landscape, and in front of you are all the goods and services you could purchase with your money. It is a world of almost infinite possibility. If you seek to fulfill your mission of increasing your financial stability, you need to find ways to direct your finite money toward those goods and services that assist you in providing for your basic needs, *before* allowing it to slip away toward your wants. Only after you have purchased the goods and services necessary to provide for these needs on an *ongoing* basis do you have extra money in your budget.

I want to emphasize: securing your basic needs does not mean you simply purchase food, clothing, and shelter themselves. You also need to purchase those items that *assist* you in securing your basic needs. The most obvious example in our society would be transportation. Most of us are not able to walk to work, which means that we need to purchase some form of transportation to be able to continue to earn money. Other examples of goods and services that support the core needs of a human are items like electricity and natural gas, both of which play a huge role in nutrition and warmth. Once again, each household's situation is unique, so what you purchase to provide food, clothing, and shelter may be very different than what other people purchase. There are no right or wrong answers here. Just keep in mind, financial stability requires you to secure your basic necessities before you spend money on other items.

At this point I expect that some of you are beginning to panic. That long-ignored klaxon in the back of your brain is getting loud enough you are no longer able to ignore it. Hang in there. Don't judge the fear that you've ignored. It was trying to tell you something, and don't judge yourself for pushing it aside. You live in a culture that told you that you were crazy. For now, let's focus on what you're going to do to plug your leaky boat.

Chapter 5:
Plugging the Leak in Your Boat

If you picture your finances as a boat, your very first task should be to make sure your boat is water-tight. You need to make sure your expenses are not greater than your income. If you are spending more than you bring in, your boat leaks and is on its way to sinking in a sea of debt. Your most important financial strategy to increase your stability is to make sure your expenses do not exceed your income. An assessment should be made on at least a monthly basis to determine if your boat leaks. In the tactics section I will show you a surefire way to keep your boat water-tight on an ongoing basis.

For now, we need to discuss what you can do if you find your boat leaking. When your expenses are greater than your income, you only have two options. You can either increase your income to cover the extra expenses, or you can reduce your expenses to a point where you can make ends meet. You might need to do a combination of the two. There really aren't any other choices. Most of the time, reducing your expenses will be the better option because consumer spending on unnecessary luxuries and status items has caused the imbalance. As much as you may want to buy a latte every day at work, that three to four dollars a day, five days a week, four weeks a month adds up to a significant amount of money. By managing these expenses in ways that bring them under control and give them boundaries, families can often find the money necessary to balance the budget and keep their boat afloat.

However, some of us will find ourselves in worse shape than eliminating lattes can solve. The first thing to do at that point will be to look again at your budget. There are probably sacred cows in your monthly expenses that you have not been willing to challenge up until now.

Until this year early fall has been a difficult time financially for my family. For the last few years my wife worked as a classroom assistant and didn't get paid during the summer months. September and October were very tight. One time when we did our September zero-based budget this year, we found we were $600 dollars short for the month. I wasn't sure what we were going to do. Finding $600 dollars to keep our boat from leaking seemed impossible. Then we went back through our budget. We eliminated literally everything that was not related to food, clothing, shelter, and transportation. We balanced our budget and kept our boat from leaking. It felt like a miracle.

It hurt to remove our charitable giving, put our gym membership on hold (which we used), and to put my student loan back in forbearance, but necessities *always* come first. We also cut items like personal care products and household cleaners to the bare minimum. Seriously consider if you have any expenses that are not related to food, clothing, shelter, and transportation. Remove them from your budget. Then see if your budget balances. I have no doubt this will hurt. On the one hand, it isn't fun at all because you are touching things that matter to you. However, there is another side to it as well. There is a joy when you find even though money is ridiculously tight you can survive without making things worse in the future by borrowing money.

Sometimes it can be very difficult to make these kinds of choices and the temptation can be very strong to just give in, borrow money, and make the pain go away. I understand that impulse. I just want to remind you if you choose to do so you are simply making things worse in the future. You might even spend yourself into a bankruptcy. Hang in there. In these circumstances, it is important to avoid borrowing money if at all possible. Find ways to increase your income if you have cut to the bone. You are not alone. I have been there with you. Even now I'm only a half step in front of you. It isn't worth it to me to enslave myself to a bank or other lender to have what I want right now.

Turning Lean Living into a Feast Instead of a Diet

Cutting all the fat and some of the meat from the budget can be a painful process, but before you despair or feel like spending less will be similar to eating a cardboard diet meal, you need to remember that your spending reflects your values. You get to decide what to spend your money on. No matter what I say in this book, you get to set your own mission. My job isn't to tell you what to do. If you want to buy stuff on credit, that won't keep me awake at night. You get to make your own choices. However, I am making an argument you will not be able to continue to seek status and entertainment in your life without risking the security of your basic needs like food, clothing, shelter, and transportation. If you think the latest Xbox will make you happier in the long term than knowing that your home is secure, then by all means get the Xbox. It's your choice.

The decision to cut expenses rather than purchase an Xbox or other item you want gets easier when you understand both activities have the same goal. Xboxes, season tickets to your favorite sports team, or whatever it is that you personally value for entertainment: these are meant to bring a sense of fun into your life. They are meant to relieve stress and increase your happiness. Yet if these things are purchased at the expense of your ability to pay your rent, they open you to huge swaths of potential unhappiness down the road. When you recognize that lean living also lowers stress and increases your sense of well-being—particularly when you suddenly find yourself in need of extra cash—then you begin to enjoy the act of putting money aside and the improved night's sleep that goes with it.

Once my brain grasped the concept that lean living brings with it lower stress, choosing to avoid spending money by cutting expenses and saving money has become a kind of game in which I find great satisfaction in spending less on something than I needed to or had budgeted. The hard work of living below your means and saving for the future provides a sense of satisfaction that can't be had from any form of entertainment or motor vehicle or whatever it is you spend money on to be happy. You just have to understand the benefits produced by the hard work.

Value "Value"

Americans undervalue products and services that help them provide for their basic needs. Since we have been able to take our basic needs for granted, we have instead invested our sense of value and worth into status and luxury goods. For instance, in my counseling practice it has not been uncommon for me to find families who spend 25 percent or more of their take-home income on transportation, simply so they could drive a certain type of car, which they perceived as giving them worth in either their own eyes or, more often, in the eyes of others. The need for a vehicle is transportation. That need could be met equally effectively at a much lower cost.

I don't like the car I drive. It's a 2000 green Chevy Astro. It's about as far from cool or sexy as you can get without a pocket protector. I would much rather be driving something curvy and sleek, but I can't find the economic value in doing so. My cost per mile would rise dramatically, even if I got better mileage. If we are going to make it our mission to use our money to preserve and increase our financial stability, we have to learn to respect and avoid choices that don't make sense financially. We also have to place a higher sense of worth on those financial choices that are smart but not sexy. We have to change the definition of a good decision. We have to value "value."

The marketing and advertising firms have so hijacked the concept of value, we often don't have a clue what is in our best interests. I can't tell you how many people I counseled that pay for a bundled cable TV package with phone and internet. Then they also pay for a full cell phone package as well. When I ask them whether or not they use the home phone, most of them say no. Yet because it came in a package that discounted the price for all three products, they paid extra to include the phone. Folks, this isn't a deal. This is paying extra for a product you don't need. So you only save 20 bucks if you get rid of the phone and purchase internet and television; that is still twenty dollars in your pocket. Cut the cable and you can often save even more.

That example is really more tactical than strategic. However, it is meant to illustrate that we have not trained ourselves to calculate the financial value of a purchase. It will take time to learn a new way to think, but the effort will protect us from huge numbers of mistakes. If you want some help with your thinking here, catch a radio program or two by Clark Howard or buy one of his books. Valuing "value" is really his area of expertise and he has loads of great advice.

I should be clear, just because you decide to consider the financial value of a product before you purchase it does not mean you must turn off your self-expression and become a faceless suburban drone who buys everything at Walmart, either. Making do with less will often allow one to purchase a fewer number of custom or high-end items. A larger number of items is not always a better deal. Simplicity helps value, as does purchasing in quantity.

Quality doesn't have to be sacrificed for the sake of choosing value either. High-quality goods and services may, in fact, be cheaper because we are often willing to pay a high price for convenience instead of quality. For example, buying and preparing quality food has been somewhat of a refuge for me in the last few years. For many years it was assumed by advocates for the poor that boxed and prepackaged foods provided a cheaper diet than fresh foods. A recent study highlighted in the New York Times finally put that myth to rest. Items like soda and prepackaged food are more expensive per serving than fresh foods. My wife and I have known this for years. Soda is expensive for the empty calories it provides, and fruits and vegetables, besides being healthy, provide a much better bang for the buck than boxed mac and cheese. I never did go for the "cheaper" argument.

So if boxed food isn't cheaper, why is it so popular? I believe it's popular because it's often more convenient. Often we pay a premium for such convenience. Boxed food versus fresh food provides only one example of the difference between convenience and value. There are others, but without going into a lot of detail let me just say, keep your eyes open and make sure you pay attention when someone tells you that an item will make your life easier. It may or may not be a good financial value.

The Other Option: Increase Your Income

Not that many years ago this section of the book would have been much easier to write and much different. I would have just told you to go out and get a second part-time job to make ends meet, but jobs aren't what they used to be. Perhaps the most significant change wrought by the Great Recession is the loss of living-wage jobs. When some of us would kill just for one middle class job but can't even find that, how can I tell people to just get another job to improve their income? When many of us are working two or three jobs and still can't make ends meet, what can I say?

Again, I come back to one of the mantras of this book. Even if right now you can't accomplish the goal, it still makes a difference if you aim at the goal. Aim at nothing, and you get nowhere. Aim at something, and even in long odds you often get closer than you would otherwise. Consider this section a reminder of what is true, not what is practical or easy today.

That said there are some signs that our job environment is beginning to improve.

In my financial counseling practice, it was not uncommon to find household budgets that were not that far from balancing, perhaps a couple of hundred dollars off. Often I suggest to these people they should consider finding part-time work to cover the gap. Some households embraced the idea. For others, I have seen monthly budget deficits of less than one hundred dollars solved through bankruptcy rather than increased income or reduced expenses. Obviously I think this is a poor choice, but sometimes we are so shell-shocked by our situation, we just want out.

On the other side, I have seen others make up thousands of dollars through increasing overtime and taking side jobs. Much depends on your determination. Remember, the easy path out isn't often the best path. Increasing income often can be a viable way to get your budget to balance.

With the job market still stacked so highly in the employers' favor, now might be a great time to start your own business. Start small, and make a little side money to help your budget balance. I think a new wave of entrepreneurship is likely to be one major means by which we change our economic reality as a country. It also may be a more viable path to increasing your income in a weak job market. I know it is the path that I am choosing this time around.

Social Services

This section will not please everyone. How could it? Some of us believe the government should provide no social safety net, and that any person who uses such services is just lazy and evil. I am not one of those people. There are good reasons for services such as food stamps and Medicaid to exist, and in dire circumstances like unemployment or true permanent disability, such payments are important for helping someone continue to survive. Because of these things, starvation does not happen in the United States unless by severe neglect of some sort. (Hunger certainly happens but not starvation, not often.) This is a good thing, and we should be proud as a country that we don't let our people suffer in that way.

If you are struggling to make ends meet right now because of low income or unemployment, you need to consider whether or not social services such as Medicaid for your health insurance would make sense. Doing so might allow you to either reduce your COBRA payment or reduce your insurance at work. Despite Obamacare, medical debt remains a leading cause for bankruptcy in the United States. State-sponsored health insurance will help. Food assistance and other services need to also be considered if you qualify.

Just one more thought before I leave this topic. When considering social services, there are two dangers, both of which can hurt your financial thinking and your long-term financial stability. Before I became a financial counselor, I was much less sympathetic to the argument that social services cause dependency. I tended to believe social services nearly always acted for good in people's lives. Yet time and time again, I had clients come into my office who felt entitled to benefits and clearly had no thought of ever trying to live without them. They had lost their shame. Really, they appeared to me to be damaged human beings who had little sense of self-worth or motivation left.

On the other hand, I also had fathers and mothers in my office who were so proud and arrogant that even though they or their children would benefit from assistance, they would not even consider it. Meanwhile they skimped on food and medicine for their family. While at least I admired their desire to live without assistance, they seem to me to have let their desire for status and self-sufficiency cloud their judgment. What good will it do your children if you get cancer and don't have insurance? How will that help them?

In the end, I think it is good to be a little embarrassed by needing assistance. This keeps you motivated to find a way to contribute taxes rather than live off others' taxes. But that should not keep you from fulfilling your moral and ethical obligations to your children. If you can get you and your family health insurance, you ought to think seriously about doing so. It will help you improve your financial stability and just might save a family member's life.

Do whatever it takes to plug the leak in your boat. Much of your success in increasing your stability will come from your dogged determination to keep your boat from leaking. Don't let anyone, not a friend, a pastor, or a politician, shame you about doing so.

For some of us it won't always be possible to fill the hole. The long history of debt shows that to be true. However, by doing everything in your power to aim toward that goal, you will find yourself much closer to financial stability than if you allow your expenses to continually exceed your income.

Chapter 6:
The Most Important Thing

Imagine for a minute it's early morning, and you are heading off to start your day. You put the key in the ignition, turn the car over, and just as you put it in gear you hear a terrible clunk. Something isn't right. There is a grinding noise and the car won't move. You manage your morning, find alternative transportation, and get your car towed to the shop. Sometime in the afternoon your phone rings. It's your mechanic. You need a new transmission. All told, a rebuilt one will be around $1,600 installed. A new one will run you just over $2,000.

Now there are two reactions possible at this point. I have had both of them at different times in my life. The more typical reaction goes something like this: "Oh, [expletive deleted]! What am I going to do? We were doing just fine until this disaster, but we don't have the money to pay for repairs; so it will have to go on a credit card, but which one? The low interest one is almost maxed already. I am going to have to put it on the high interest card. We'll never pay it off. That card is over 20 percent. I hope we can make the payment." These thoughts are accompanied by a growing feeling of dread, fear, and the knowledge you will have to tell your significant other.

Compare that reaction to this one: "I can't believe we have the money in the bank for this! I don't even have to worry about paying the bill. This feels great! I want to feel this way every time we have a problem." The first time you use your emergency fund, you forget all about the fact that you have to pay for a car repair. You walk in to the mechanic, and he starts getting suspicious because you are smiling as you fork over 1,600 bucks. It's a good moment.

Experiencing the contrast between moments like these two has been one of the most important reasons I have become so doggedly determined to avoid debt. The first situation is just miserable. The second has the tendency to turn lemons into lemonade. Savings provides the means to make that transition.

Protect Your Future Stability

More than any other necessary item, people forget to purchase future stability in their budget. Even households without extravagant expenses forget to purchase stability in the future. At some point in time, your monthly expenses or income will change suddenly; perhaps you will have a car accident; God forbid, your partner will suddenly get cancer or you will lose your job. We may not know which financial disaster will land at our door, but we do know, some kind of financial disaster will come.

Beyond actual food, clothing, shelter, and everything needed to support those necessities, an emergency fund is the single most important item to purchase in a household budget.

Yet in many households their credit card is their emergency plan. This is a very poor plan that often turns what is a small emergency in the moment into a financial crisis down the road.

In many households, emergencies like the transmission repair described above are handled in the following manner. The car breaks down. The repair costs $600. Since the household has no savings, a credit card is used to pay for the repairs. A typical payout at a reasonable 12 percent interest rate, using minimum payments, would take nearly five years to pay off and cost around $170.00 in interest. If your interest rates are at a penalty rate of 21.9 percent, you would pay nearly $459 dollars of interest over six years, making the actual cost of the car repair over $1,000! Multiply this figure by several occurances each year, and it becomes clear, many families are losing hundreds of dollars each year on emergency interest alone.

Now imagine what happens to a family without savings in a large-scale emergency? What if someone gets laid off? With an all-too-common large-scale emergency, things quickly spiral out of control, and the family suddenly faces some very tough choices, like giving up their home or filing for bankruptcy.

Now what happens if the same family prepays for their inevitable car repair or layoff with savings? First of all, they instantly put all the interest back in their pockets, leaving them money for a nice trip each summer. More importantly, the emergency does not automatically change their monthly expenses. Next month they don't have any extra payments. Because of these two benefits, they have a much greater financial stability than the household that has no savings and uses its credit card for an emergency.

I recognize that many of you will think it is not possible to actually pay for savings each month. You will say that your budget can't handle it. For some of you this may be true. There are times when you may not be able to put any money aside. For some of us, including myself in the last couple of years, putting all our income toward securing our food, clothing, and shelter leaves literally nothing left over. I want to affirm, you are doing a great job with your finances. Financial stability is much more about doing the best with what you have and not about achieving a certain level of income. Yet the harsh reality is that you may be doing the best you can and still end up with debt in an emergency. If at all possible, find a way to squeeze more blood from the turnip and put away some money—even ten or twenty dollars a month can make a big difference in a small emergency.

However, for most of my readers this isn't the case. For most of us, we are happy paying interest and ignoring our need for savings. We happily pay a two-hundred-dollar cable bill and pay for unlimited data on our cell phone without hesitation while failing to put anything away for the future. We pay extra on our credit cards each month because we want to relieve the pressure, but we don't put any money away. Then when the next emergency comes, we use our credit cards again. What a vicious cycle! For the majority of us, the reality is, we *can* afford savings. We just don't want to change our lifestyle to have better security. In that case, we need to quit saying we can't afford to save. Instead, we need to be more honest with ourselves about what we truly value. (I will give you a hint. If you are paying for cable and not saving for an emergency, you value cable more than you value your ability to pay for food, clothing, and shelter for your family.)

Why Saving Matters Even When You Can't

I can hear some of you right now getting ready to close the book in frustration. Saving money seems to be out of reach. For some of you it truly is out of reach. If you are not able to save right now, I want to reaffirm that this book and these ideas are still for you (and me). The most important factor to growing your financial stability isn't your income. Rather, your success is much more related to how well you keep your eye on the ball. Organize your finances around the principles of financial stability. Aim for that goal and over time you will find many unexpected ways to actually put money aside.

During the Great Recession, while I walked through one difficult career change after another, I cannot tell you how many times I had money in the bank, even large sums, only to see it used up in the next emergency. At times I had debt as well. We weren't always able to keep our nose above water. We used tax returns to pay off two hospital bills that had been sent to collections because we had not been able to pay them. There were a couple of times we had to ask others for help. Recently, we've been able to start to give a little back, and I fully intend to replicate the generosity I received during our lean years. It was rough, but we are still standing today because we knew where to set our compass, and we are dogged in following that path.

For those of you still in the middle of the pain, don't quit! If you give up and give in to your impulses, things may go from frustrating but livable to disastrous. For those of you who are truly living hand to mouth, the goal of this chapter is to give you something to aim at. You may not be able to put much money away right now, but when your tax return comes in, rather than spending it on new stuff this year, it will be time to put $1,000 aside for emergencies and use the rest to pay down debt.

From Slush Fund to Designated Funds: How to Grow Your Savings

Healthy financial planning is three parts science and two parts art. The number of financial decisions we face on a daily and weekly basis makes knowing just what should be done in any situation almost impossible. Looking back, I wonder if we could have been saving money when I could find hundreds to cut to make my budget balance each fall. Yet, at the time we were already skimping, and I judged our choices as all being necessary. It takes practice to develop the instincts necessary to make good financial decisions. Also, healthy financial thinking integrates several different skill sets together to create a whole. You need to know when to spend money and when to save it. You need to understand the relative value of the product you want to purchase. You also need to be able to resist your cravings, among other skills. Often weaving the pieces together well is as important as knowing what pieces should be part of our plan. For instance, most of us know that we need a savings account, and many of us have tried to put money away previously, only to see it disappear when the next serious consumer craving comes along. Savings has to be part of an overall set of strategies that lead toward the goal of financial stability. I want to take a minute to talk about how to integrate savings into your financial road map so it meshes with your other strategies for creating stability.

I have argued the first and most important savings in any plan to move toward financial stability should be a $1,000 emergency fund. An emergency fund acts as a bulwark against debt, and debt represents the greatest threat to your financial stability. Without an emergency fund, it will be nearly impossible for you to pay for unexpected expenses such as home repairs or car repairs without using debt.

An emergency fund represents a key missing ingredient in most plans to pay off debt. For most of us, when we are feeling the pressure from our debt, we become desperate to get that pressure off our back. We want it gone now. So when we get some extra money, for instance, a tax return, we tend to instantly throw it at debt. However, since most of us have no savings whatsoever, we quickly end up right back in debt when the next financial problem arises. So by saving an emergency fund *before* paying more than minimum payments on any debt, we greatly increase our chances of paying off debt, long term, and staying debt-free.

At first, your savings acts as a kind of slush fund. Its main purpose is to fill the gaps when your *needs* are greater than your income. It is truly for emergencies.

Down the road, when we've worked hard on paying off our consumer debts, the most immediate threat to a family's financial situation has been eliminated. At this point, the role of savings changes and gets more complex. Savings remains a household's first defenses against unexpected expenses, such as layoffs. Increasing the emergency fund from $1,000 to eight-to-ten-months of expenses needs to be a high priority.

However, after debts are paid off, there should now be extra money in the budget, and before it gets blown on consumer junk, we need to make sure that we take care of other regular, long-term expenses. First and foremost, these are transportation expenses. Your vehicle will wear out someday. Borrowing for a new car is probably one of the most common poor financial choices we make, and we'll talk more about it later. If we are going to avoid this problem, it will be necessary to save some money each month for a new car.

Savings now changes from the slush fund approach, in which your most important goal was to pay off your consumer debts, and moves to more of a designated funds kind of model, in which even if there is only one savings account, these funds are intended for more than one purpose. If that gets too complicated, I suggest keeping at least your emergency fund in a separate account—at another bank if necessary—to make sure it still exists when you need it. During this phase of our financial growth, the emergency fund is still growing toward that eight-to-ten months of expenses, but now we are also saving for items such as a new vehicle, and we might even begin to save for a vacation that will be paid for with cash. (Imagine what it will feel like to come home from a vacation without worrying about how you are going to make your credit card payment. Won't that be great!)

How detailed you want to be with accounting for each separate savings item is somewhat a matter of personal style. I tend to do better with a few large categories that are used for all long-term expenses with highly specific small categories for short-term wants like vacations. However, you cannot be too careful here. It would really not be helpful to have spent the savings on a new kitchen only to end up needing a new car shortly thereafter. Designating funds helps to make sure these kinds of problems are avoided and helps make it clear, especially early on, what you can actually afford to spend on a given item. Also, don't forget that your core mission is to secure your basic needs. Don't let saving for extras eat into either that mission or your dedication.

Saving for Retirement

This isn't a book on planning for retirement. Actually, that isn't quite true. This isn't a book that is directly about how to save for retirement. However, anyone who aims at financial stability is much more likely to be ready for retirement than someone who arrives at its door with credit card debt and 20 plus years to go on their mortgage. Just think how much less you have to save if you don't have any debt, and you own your house free and clear. It will make the burden of saving for retirement much simpler.

Even though this book won't cover the hows and whys of mutual funds and financial advisers, it is worth mentioning a few things before we move on. First, it doesn't make sense to be saving for retirement if you are going in the hole each month. Remember, your first priority is to make sure on a monthly basis that your boat is not leaking. If you can't pay for your basic necessities right now, you have no business trying to pay for them in the future.

Next, retirement savings is not as high a priority as making sure that you pay off your debts right now. Debt is a risk and remains an ongoing threat to your household until it is paid off. Even if your boat is stable at this point in time, what would happen if you were suddenly to lose your job? You could end up in a position where you can no longer pay for your credit cards, and if it takes too long to find another job, you may end up in a bankruptcy. If you end up in a bankruptcy, there is a good chance your creditors will try to take your retirement funds to pay for your debts.

In some cases, it makes sense to stop making your retirement contributions to pay off your debt, even if it means giving up a company match. Remember, our goal here isn't to become wealthy but instead to be financially stable. What good is the company match if you end up in a situation in which you are bankrupt and have your retirement taken away anyway? Retirement savings shouldn't be allowed to threaten your financial stability, no matter how enticing the free money offered by your company. (Remember that the match isn't truly free. There is a cost—five years of loyalty to a company that may or may not be a good fit for you.)

Once your consumer debts have been paid off, by all means take that company match. (In fact, if you have your consumer debts paid off, why aren't you taking your full company match?) However, beyond that, keep your contributions modest until you have a full emergency fund of eight to ten months. Remember, a fully funded emergency fund is necessary to keep you from losing your home if you are suddenly unemployed. That takes a higher priority than a retirement fund.

On the other hand, many of us don't really have a problem of placing too high a priority on saving for retirement. Most of us actually are saving too little and spending the extra on other things. Here is a good rule of thumb: between 10 and 15 percent of your earnings should be saved for retirement each month. However, something is always better than nothing, so save what you can.

In the last several chapters we have talked a lot about expenses and how savings can help you in a pinch, but we haven't yet spent any real time talking about debt. Going into debt of all sorts is so common in our culture, it's worth taking a hard look at when, if ever, debt is helpful. That will be the topic for our next chapter.

Strategy Number 1
Live Below Your Means and Save the Extra

Rainy days come for all of us. I doubt anyone ever looked back and said, "I over-prepared for that one." Our pursuit of status instead of stability has left many people shell-shocked and traumatized now that the day of reckoning has arrived. Back at the beginning of our section on strategies, I said many people still immigrate to the United States for the unprecedented economic opportunity. I have had the privilege of helping a few of these immigrants figure out how to live in our economic system. Often they find themselves baffled by our easy credit, and soon they are over their head in debt. When I ask them whether or not in their old country they would have borrowed money like they did, invariably they said, "No." They assumed because this was America somehow the rules of good finance had changed. I often ended up telling them to go back to their old thinking when it came to money: make sure your needs are taken care of, then save for a rainy day. They often nodded in understanding. I didn't worry too much about those clients. They had a wealth of cultural experience they could draw on to make wise decisions in the future.

The best way to increase your chances of weathering a financial storm without any damage is to simply live below your means and save some of the rest. It is a practice that has been followed for centuries around the world. It's time we learned that the same rules still apply here as well.

Chapter 7:
Financial Nukes

So I am definitely pushing our military metaphors a bridge too far here (get it?), but, in certain ways, a credit card reminds me of a nuke. As a refresher, let me remind you we have been looking at useful strategies to implement that can help us all achieve the mission of financial stability. In military thinking, the President determines the mission, and the military decides on the strategies necessary to accomplish the mission. The daily activities they use to carry out their strategies are called tactics. This kind of thinking makes almost all weapons tactical. They are the means by which the military implements their strategies—and then there are nukes.

The use of these weapons at the end of World War II moved beyond a mere tactic of battle, they became a strategy to end the war. The use of a nuke to accomplish the President's goals became a strategy in itself: thus the term, "strategic weapons."

The problem with nukes and other strategic weapons is that they come with all sorts of crazy consequences that are not very healthy for the planet or the soul of the nation which uses them. One horrific example would be the callous deaths of hundreds of thousands of civilians along the way to accomplishing the surrender of Japan.

All of these features of a nuclear weapon tend to remind me of credit cards and other consumer-debt products. Credit cards, in particular, have the power to instantly change any financial situation and make it *feel* better for the cardholder, because they end the pain in that moment. If I don't have enough money to pay my phone bill, pull out the credit card. If I don't have enough money to pay for food, pull out the credit card. If I cannot live without spending at least $900 on Christmas gifts each year, pull out the credit card. (Around $900 is the average amount families in the United States report spending on Christmas presents.) In fact, credit cards are so powerful at changing any financial decision-making process, for many households they are no longer even considered a tactic to be used at the appropriate time (is there one?); they have become a strategy used for survival. Yet they and other debt products have all sorts of toxic effects on our financial behavior. Worse yet, when a household begins to see them as necessary for everyday living, they shape and change that household's financial thinking in ways that are highly self-destructive.

Credit Cards and Conditioning: Getting Used to Taking Bad Bets

The credit card is an amazingly efficient tool for changing our financial thinking and teaching us to take unnecessary risks, because the first bet rarely, if ever, goes bad. Since the first bet appears to have worked, we make another and another and another. After a while, we become conditioned to making bets with our money. Only after we have made many bets do we find ourselves in financial trouble. By that point, the "better" lifestyle the credit card seemed to provide is far out of reach, because the debt-service payments take so much of our income.

To cure the problem, we would have to adopt a lifestyle that is below even our current diminished expectations, and that is too painful for many people. We find ourselves afraid of doing without our debt, and our credit card has become a source of comfort and solace in our disappointment.

It does amaze me how many people walked into my financial counseling office and had no concept that they didn't need to own a credit card. By the time they were in financial trouble, their credit card was such an ingrained part of their financial existence they were unable to remember life without it. They were terrified they would not be safe unless they had at least one credit card for emergencies. For many, their first credit card came when they were in college, and there had been no adult financial life without one. Like an abused spouse, they didn't recognize that their credit card was the source of their misery. Instead, they felt emotionally attached to it. They got defensive and misty-eyed if I suggested they go without it. (Come on folks! You're in love with a credit card? Really?)

Many of these consumers go along quite successfully for a while. They reach a balance point between their debt-service payments and their incomes. The banks love these households because they no longer have any hope or intention of trying to pay off their debt. They are rewarded with high credit scores, which they then work very hard to maintain. Yet, each month their budget feels like a stretch because they have just enough money for their basic necessities and their debt-service payment.

They don't yet feel the true pain of their situation because new extras go onto the credit card. They don't realize if they simply purchased the same items but paid cash, they would have much more money to spend simply by avoiding the interest payment on their credit cards.

Often the best way for this kind of consumer to understand what their credit cards cost them is for them to look at the amount of money they would have in their pocket each month without a credit card payment. The truth is, most often these households do not have an income problem. They have plenty of money. Instead, their debt-service payments send huge chunks of money into other people's pockets.

Let's once again imagine standing with last month's earnings in hand and all that you could do with those earnings spread out before you. Now, I want you to see yourself taking a large wad of that money out of your own hand and walking away with it into the past. This is what happens when we use a credit card. We take from our future selves, to have what we want in the present. What makes this even worse is that we *pay* for the privilege of robbing ourselves in the future. Households that use credit cards pay hundreds of dollars annually for the privilege of having a worse lifestyle in the future. What an amazing scam!

If you want to surprise yourself, go and add up all the credit card interest you paid last year. Then consider what kind of vacation you could have bought your family with that same money. As I said earlier, human desire is an unquenchable ocean. Once you let it control your finances, many foolish choices become possible.

Leverage: The Other Side of the Coin

I am not alone in my assessment of credit card debt. There are many writers, authors, and speakers in the personal finance world who also stress debt reduction and elimination as the best way to increase your family's financial stability, Dave Ramsey and Suze Orman being particularly passionate examples. Unfortunately, we do not control the culture, and we probably never will. Debt is big business in the United States. There is too much money to be made by selling debt to you. Of course, there are those who make highly effective and compelling arguments that debt is a normal part of human existence and paying interest to someone else should be part of every family's strategy for managing their money.

It is worth noting, a majority of these proponents of personal debt benefit in some way by keeping you in debt. For instance, most financial advisers make a commission off the products they sell, or they make a percentage of the assets they manage. Either way, this gives them a vested interest in arguing you should keep your debt and use your savings instead to purchase the various financial products they sell. It makes them money. Again, let me remind you that business people, including financial advisers, are very serious about what they do. I know: I was a financial adviser for a while. For them, selling you a financial product means the difference between making their mortgage payment and losing their home. Because they take it so seriously, it is worth taking a moment and considering some of their arguments.

Like all effective arguments, it begins with a piece of the truth. Debt can provide the ability to make your money do more for you than you could otherwise. In the financial world, this is called leverage. This is mathematically possible. According to many financial advisers, my bank, and the car dealer if I have $10,000 and need a car, I should not pay cash for the vehicle. Rather, I should borrow the money for my vehicle and use that money to do other work for me. For instance, a financial adviser will point out that if I borrow for a vehicle at 5 percent for six years and invest in a mutual fund that has averaged an 8 percent return over the last ten years, then I will come out better in the end. (Of course, this is assuming you do invest that $10,000 and don't just spend it right away.)

The math says so, doesn't it? Sure it does. If I put no money down and borrowed at 5 percent on the vehicle, I would make payments of $157.16 each month and pay a total of $11,316. So the cost of the vehicle is $11,316. During the same time frame, I would earn 8 percent on my money and make $15,869. That means at the end of the six year time frame, I have $4,553 that I wouldn't have had if I had paid cash for the vehicle. That's a lot of money, isn't it? What's not to like?

What's not to like is all the financial risk that this simple math does not calculate into this scenario. Let's start with the easiest risk to spot. If your mutual fund has given you an 8 percent return for the last ten years, will it give you that return for the next six? There is no way to know. Really that depends on the stock or bond markets. It depends on the economy for the next six years. It depends on the wisdom of the people managing the mutual fund in the next six years. There is no way to tell. What can be said is that for the last ten years the people who bet their money with this mutual fund received an 8 percent return. That is so very different than saying you *will* get a better return if you borrow on the vehicle and purchase a mutual fund with the money.

Please don't get me wrong, I think that mutual funds are great investments, and I suggest that when you save for retirement you use them wisely. However, right now we are trying to determine whether or not you should use them to make money while you borrow on a vehicle. That is a different story, and the return on the investment isn't the only risk that you take when you use leverage.

Next, one must consider the risk to your finances of the payment. For the next six years your budget needs to be able to tolerate another $157 a month in payments. No matter what anyone says, it is not possible to predict the future six years from now. What might be affordable today, might not be affordable tomorrow. So now we have two risks, which we must calculate to understand how they affect our choice to borrow money rather than pay cash for a vehicle.

The final risk, which must always be considered when one is going to borrow money, is the risk of default. That is, what happens if you cannot pay. What happens if in the next six years you lose your job? What kinds of stress will you face then, compared to if you had paid cash? If you lose your job, not only do you have to worry about food, clothing, and shelter, but now your transportation is also under threat. That is one more stress that you don't need.

Do you know what happens when you do not pay on your car? It gets repossessed and then sold. You still owe the difference between its selling price and your outstanding debt, which shouldn't be that much if you have a decent loan, right? Wrong. When your vehicle gets repossessed, they sell it at about 25 to 30 cents on the dollar. If the retail value is $8,000 and you owe $10,000, you end up with a collections bill between $7,600 and $8,000 on a vehicle that you no longer own!

So now you have to find alternative transportation so you can keep working to support you family, and you have another $8,000 in debt to add to your credit card bills. Double that if you borrowed $20,000 so you could drive that Prius. I shudder to think about how much you would owe if you borrowed $30,000 plus for that *new* SUV with the built-in DVD player you "needed" for your children.

Few people consider these risks before they go borrow money to purchase a car, and even fewer people recognize that these risks are cumulative. That is, each risk happens independently of the others. In other words, all three of the risks listed above might come true at once. More importantly, since they act independently of each other, you need to add them together to get a true picture of whether or not this plan will succeed. In other words, if there is a 20 percent risk that your mutual fund bet won't work and a 15 percent risk that you might lose your job, plus approximately another 10 percent risk of default, then what was a sure thing when you did the math suddenly only has a 61 percent chance of success. Doesn't sound like such a good deal any more, does it? This is especially true when you calculate in the extra stress on the finances created each month by your car payments, which for some of you can be upwards of $700 to $900 per month for two vehicles! (I know, I've seen household budgets just like yours.)

I don't know what the exact risk of failure is on this kind of a car loan bet. It probably isn't as high as I made it. But the truth is, it is nearly impossible to calculate and failure can't be calculated by just the repossessions. There are a huge number of people who make their payments but are suffering horribly for their decision to take on debt. They may be skimping on other items or unable to pay their mortgage. Or simply, their mutual funds may be way down while they are paying interest on the car. They have lost their leverage bet.

Before you waste your time either feeling dumb (or macho) about your ability to calculate risk, remember even the math Ph.D.s at AIG, Bear Sterns, Lehman Brothers, and the like couldn't calculate risk. They were making bad bets just like you and me. Frankly, there is more and more scientific evidence to show human beings don't calculate risk well.

A January 2008 blog post titled, "10 Ways We Get the Odds Wrong" on psychologytoday.com highlighted at least ten reasons human beings are so poor at estimating risk:

1. Human beings allow their emotions to influence their risk assessments.
2. We fear spectacular but unlikely events more than we ought.
3. We underestimate risks that creep up on us over the long term.
4. We prefer control even if it increases risk.
5. We substitute one risk for another and believe we are safer.
6. Teens overthink risks, rather than trusting their instincts.
7. Our gender, stage of life, and other social factors help determine our tolerance for risk.
8. Risk assessments are influenced by our values.
9. We accept "natural" risks more readily than we accept "human created" risks.
10. Worry itself increases our risk for health problems like heart-disease. (In other words, the fear of risk increases our risk.)

Our difficulty calculating risk is why I believe if financial stability is your goal, then debt should be avoided if at all possible. I would rather drive an old jalopy than borrow money for the status of having a car payment. I would rather have to wait a couple of months to save the money before spending a weekend away with my wife rather than pay interest on it later. Don't get me wrong; I am not someone who is cheap. I love nice things, and I hate my 2000 Chevy Astro. But every time I do the math on whether or not it is worth it to purchase something different, it never makes sense to me. My current car runs great, and frankly not having a payment provides so much financial stability to my children, I can't see doing otherwise. I still hate the car though.

Admitting that you are not qualified to calculate risk takes humility. It also takes the ability to be countercultural. We love to tell the stories of the winners. Lottery winners make the papers. Lottery losers don't. We love to tell the story of the stock broker who slept in a bathroom with his son while in training and then got his Lamborghini. We don't like to tell the story of the six other guys who worked just as hard and ended up homeless. That's kind of a downer. If we are going to get over our obsession with wealth and status to find financial stability, we have to be willing to tell more honest stories, and we have to be willing to be humble enough to avoid unnecessary risk for the sake of status.

What to Do If You Are in Credit Card Trouble

Some of you are out there saying, "Enough already! I know I'm in trouble. I just want to know what to do about it. That's why I picked up the book!" Thanks for your patience while I brought some of your fellow readers along. So what do you do if you find yourself in financial trouble? What can you do about your credit card payments? Once again, credit cards open you up to a lot of poor financial thinking, so one of the best things you can do is to slow down and think through your choices before you make any decisions. Quick decisions tend to be bad decisions.

If you're serious about solving your problem, you must be radically honest with yourself. First off, you need to know whether your boat is leaking on a monthly basis and how badly. You need to understand if your monthly spending is outstripping your income. Remember, it does little good to take the water out of the boat if you still have a leak. In the tactics section I will talk about a very simple ways to know if you are making it on a month-to-month basis. For now, just remember your first step is to find out how bad your problem really is.

For many households, an analysis of income and expenses will reveal simple lifestyle changes that will take care of the problem. For these households, they need to take the extras out of the budget, and then follow the financial road map laid out in a couple of chapters.

For other households, the situation is more desperate. They may already be at a skin-and-bones budget, and just barely get by with their credit card payments. There may not be any more fat to trim. These households need to consider some outside help to solve their problem. There are places to go, and there are places not to go, for that help.

One tactic many consumers try at this point in their financial death spiral is to call their credit card companies. If they have a good payment history, they may be able to get from these companies some kind of temporary lower rate and payment to help them get back on their feet. These arrangements have the advantage of keeping the credit card open, which helps minimize the damage to the credit score, but most often these efforts do not work.

Typically, when a family needs to use one of these plans, they are already at the point where they have very little available in their budget to throw at their credit card. So the credit card company reduces the interest rate, *and* they reduce the payment. The family under stress quickly accepts the lower payment because it reduces the strain on their budget. Now the credit card company has them trapped. They now have some relief for the year they are offered the reduced payment. However, they make very little progress on their overall debt. Their lower payment doesn't allow them to reduce their principal balance much at all. At the end of the year, the credit card company simply puts their interest rate back to where it was. The stress returns, and the family has made little headway. In these scenarios, they are not very likely to actually pay off their debts, and this is just what the credit card company wants. The bank has maintained their hold on the consumer's pocketbook, allowing them to continue to extract money from the consumer to give to their stockholders.

Another trap many families fall into when trying to dig out from credit card debt is the for-profit debt consolidation industry. Frankly, I think this industry should either be outlawed as a scam or highly regulated with disclosure rules. In most cases, their business model works in the following manner. The panicked consumer walks in the door, and the salesman offers a miraculous payment for all their credit card debts, a payment that is significantly below their minimum payments. The grateful consumer signs up for the plan without understanding the for-profit company is well aware the consumer is in trouble. Once again, they are business people and take their own existence seriously. So they do what any wise business would do when working with people who are almost bankrupt. They make sure to take their own cut first. So the consumer pays their consolidated bill and doesn't realize that for the first six months or so the for-profit company doesn't pay a cent to the credit card companies. Then after that six month period in which the credit card company prepares to write off the debt, the debt consolidation company negotiates a settlement with the credit card company that pays much less than the borrower actually owes. All the while the consumer often has no idea what has happened. They are assuming that their credit cards are being paid each month.

While I am not a big fan of worshiping your credit score, I don't see any reason to needlessly damage it either. Not paying your bills for six months isn't exactly easy on the credit score, and paying an amount which is less than the full amount you borrowed looks to many lenders like a kind of bankruptcy. Late payments or non-payments are bad enough, but when you don't make good on the debt in the end, that really doesn't look good. I doubt that most consumers intend to sign up for this kind of damage when they walk into a debt consolidation office. Then there is the matter of the profit the company extracts for providing a questionable service.

A better option for consumers struggling with consumer debt is to look for a non-profit credit counseling agency accredited by the National Foundation for Credit Counseling (NFCC). If possible, I encourage you to find a local office you can deal with on a face-to-face basis. This will help you avoid scams and give you a place to go to have your questions answered. The NFCC can be found online at nfcc.org. The 800 number to call for assistance is listed at the top of their page.

The credit counseling agencies accredited by the NFCC offer debt management programs that repay 100 percent of what a consumer owes in a five-year time frame, and they negotiate with creditors to get permanently lowered interest rates for the consumer. In return, the consumer agrees to do two things. First, they agree to a fixed consolidated payment. Second, consumers also agree to close credit cards paid by the program, so they cannot run up further debts causing larger losses for the credit card companies.

In most cases a debt management plan is much more modest on the consumer's credit score than the for-profit debt consolidation plans. There is some effect because when a consumer closes credit cards, their available credit drops while their amount borrowed stays steady. This increases the ratio of amount borrowed to available credit. Credit rating agencies consider a borrower who has borrowed almost up to the limits of their available credit to be much greater risks than borrowers who have large amounts of available credit. However, unlike for-profit debt consolidation, this problem will cure itself as the debt management program goes along. The debts are paid down, and the ratio improves along with the credit score.

Again, if you are facing this kind of credit card problem, the chances of escaping without damage to your credit score are about zero, so definitely seek the help you need, even if it hurts your score in the short term. Besides, if you are committing to living in a more financially stable way in the future, you won't be borrowing money anyway, so what does your credit score matter? Now that's a new thought, isn't it? Remember credit score worship is just one way banks continue to take your money and give it to their stockholders. I'll let you in on a secret. I haven't checked my credit score in years. I don't need to. I have a home and I pay cash for cars. Why do I care about my credit score?

Finally, for some consumers it will become clear they have exhausted all their options. On a month-to-month basis they can no longer make ends meet and pay their debt bills. At this point in time, it would be wise for them to discuss their options with a bankruptcy attorney. Remember, as with any other good or service, you get what you pay for, so make sure you interview several attorneys and find the one who makes you the most comfortable. When it comes to legal matters, cheapest isn't always the best value.

So is that end of the story about debt? Just don't, ever? Not quite; there are a few circumstances in which the leverage argument can make sense, and these will be the subject of our next chapter. For now however, I want you to remember debt always adds uncertainty to any situation, and most often it makes you poorer in the future. So if our mission is to increase our stability, then in almost all circumstances, debt should simply be avoided.

Chapter 8:
Tactical Nukes

Inevitably the question arises, are there ever times when borrowing money *might* be OK? The short answer is: it depends. How is that for my best imitation of an attorney? There are certainly times when the risk of a given debt might be worth considering. Debt does have the power to allow the borrower to do things they couldn't otherwise afford. Leverage can work. Yet, if financial stability is our goal, it is almost always better to use cash if it keeps us out of debt, because debt always introduces risk to any given situation.

The only exception that comes to mind is if using cash will greatly increase your chances of going into debt later. For example, it wouldn't be wise to use your emergency fund to pay for your child's college if it makes it likely that your next unexpected expense will go on a credit card. In this case, a student loan might be a better option.

So when is debt OK to consider, and when is it not OK? First of all, debt is never useful just to fulfill a simple human want. So we are not discussing, "When is it OK to put my cruise on credit?" Using debt to purchase consumer goods or services is *never* a wise financial decision. Debt is only worth considering when it has the potential to pay for itself and give you a tangible (and occasionally intangible) return for the risk. In other words, the debt must be an investment.

Investments are always a game of risk. When I purchase a stock, I am betting that sometime in the future that stock will be worth more than what I paid for it. When I purchase a bond, I am betting the borrower will have the cash flow to continue to pay back their debt to me. Investments are risks. It is the risk in the investment that causes it to pay you more than you put in. The larger the risk, the higher the potential payout should be to compensate for the risk. If a debt is large but only offers small reward, then that debt is not worth taking.

The problem here is most of us purchase our investments like we purchase consumer goods. If it feels right, we do it. Purchasing investments needs to be a more considered process than listening CNBC all day. (You laugh, but some of you still get your investment advice from television and wouldn't know how to analyze a stock or mutual fund if your retirement depended on it, and it does.) Having said that, there are three different circumstances that come to mind in which it might be worth borrowing money. Each of them is worth looking at individually.

Student Loans

American dependency on debt starts early. In fact some of the very earliest decisions we make as young eighteen-year-old adults lead to massive amounts of debt, which haunt many of us for decades. The decision to go to college can do more financial damage than any other decision a young person makes. Don't get me wrong, I think that college is a good thing if done properly. I just don't believe a bachelor's degree that comes at a price tag of forty or fifty thousand in student loan debt is *always* a good value.

The issues here are complex, and I am hesitant to try to set out principles that may or may not work in a given circumstance, but I am confident enough to say that student loans need to provide a clear return on the investment, because they will likely be the second largest debt a person gets in their life. On top of that, the federal government, in its wisdom, has declared that in most circumstances a borrower cannot remove student loan debt with a bankruptcy, so the student will have to pay it off no matter what their financial situation. Taken together, these facts show young adults need to start asking serious questions about the value of their student-loan before they accept it.

In a job market where wages are stagnant at best and more likely sinking, is it really worth it to go deeply in debt for a degree that doesn't offer a clear path to higher wages on the other side? With the rising cost of tuition and the rising amounts of debt taken per student, it is certainly time to have such a conversation. However, a good friend of mine who is a college professor in Kentucky made a compelling case that the degree isn't as important as the actual formation of the person that takes place through getting the degree, and I would agree with him: this formation can be very compelling and useful for young adults. College teaches many valuable things that are not on the diploma. However, does a more expensive private college provide such a vastly greater number of these developmental experiences to justify the cost when compared to a significantly cheaper state school? Perhaps, but maybe not.

Again, I don't think there is any easy answer here. That isn't the point. Rather, as in all our financial thinking, the question of the relative value of one type of college education and degree over another has not often been asked. A friend of my wife decided she was not going to borrow to get her teaching degree. It took her more years to complete than her colleagues, and she got her degree from a local state university, so the degree has no prestige associated with it. Frankly, it left her lower on the totem pole when the downturn came. In the union-controlled, seniority-driven world of the teaching profession, she has struggled to keep a job as a middle-school math teacher. However, she doesn't have any debt, and unlike many others of her cohort who do have debt, she doesn't have student loan payments to consider while looking for work. This is allowing her to get by while others flounder. Once again, debt, even "good" debt, always adds risks to any situation and less risk is almost always the better way to go.

Considering the value of a degree doesn't always mean cheaper is better either. If you know exactly what you want to do, if you have examined your field and know your degree will provide employment, if both of these are true and you get into an Ivy-League quality school, by all means take the debt. These schools clearly offer intangible opportunities like no other, and in most cases the risk will be worth it. But if you are paying private-school tuition to earn even a decent regional degree in a profession that offers little stable employment, I think you have to truly ask yourself whether or not the extra intangibles at such a school outweigh the extra debt compared to a state school. Again, I am not against a college education. I have a couple of degrees myself, both from private colleges. However, I do think with rising tuition and sinking wages the question of value must come into play when we consider education for a young person. We can no longer take such questions for granted.

There is one other quick thing I want to mention about school debt before moving on. The question of value is even more important for an adult. When I was a financial counselor, I saw many adults come into my office saying they had been laid off, and they were going back to school to get a degree because there were no jobs available to them. In many cases, they were using student loans to buy food, clothing, shelter, and transportation while they studied. Here is the kicker: most of the time, the retraining they were going through would not generate enough of a pay raise on the other end to make the amount of debt worth it. I have met massage therapists who had tens of thousands of dollars in debt for both their student loans and getting their business started. This makes no sense financially whatsoever when you actually look at both the average burnout rate and average wage of a massage therapist.

I believe some of these folks don't know what to do to find a job that pays a living wage, so they are sitting in school until inspiration strikes them. I would argue this is not a good choice at all. Most of the time, they have not cut their budgets to the bone; instead they are using their college aid just like a credit card. Now that isn't smart! At least with a credit card if disaster strikes you can go through bankruptcy and remove the debt. Professional students will have to pay back their student loans no matter what. Especially as an older adult, you better be very sure your degree will offer you a viable path to a better income before you take on student loan debt.

By the way, when researching the value of a possible degree, don't take the word of the college for it either. Do your own research to make sure there is a job for you after you get your marine biology or history degree. Remember, diplomas and education are products like other products, and colleges are in the business of selling them, even if they don't serve your needs. They take their job seriously, and if they can entice you to plunk down fifty grand for a bachelors degree in fifteenth-century Turkish music, they will do it without hesitation and without any sense of moral obligation to find you a job later. Do you take your financial stability seriously? Then you better know your student loan debt will pay off.

Business Debt

Once we get out of school and find out what corporate America is really like, many of us are tempted to open our own businesses, something college has not trained us to do well. This now becomes the second time when some of us consider borrowing money, whether it is an SBA (Small Business Administration) loan or a loan from a relative.

How to open a business and when to use debt in a business context are the subject of many books and, frankly, not my area of expertise. However, in most circumstances at the beginning of a business, business debt is personally guaranteed by the owner. In this case, it really doesn't matter if the payment comes from your business checking account (you do have one of those, right?); that debt is your personal debt, and you will pay it even if the business goes under. If we are concerned with the stability of our finances for our family, adding a whole bunch of debt that might or might not get paid based upon the success of a business isn't helpful.

Once again, we have to ask some serious questions about both risk and value. Make sure you seriously consider both the likely return on your investment and more importantly, the various risks that must be taken to get that return. Once both of these questions have been considered, you must make a serious analysis of whether the amount of debt you must take to get that return is worth it. Making this kind of analysis can be very tricky, especially if you are considering purchasing an existing business, a franchise opportunity, or another "prepackaged" business.

Remember, the seller has a vested interest in downplaying the risks and exaggerating the returns. I have had several friends get in trouble because they have taken sellers at their word, purchased franchises or businesses, and ended up with much more modest returns than promised. This leaves them working long hours for very little return and in deep personal debt to boot.

Many new business owners mingle their business finances and personal finances. In many ways I understand this mistake. Most of us are deeply invested in our businesses, and at the beginning, our income and expenses can be irregular and sporadic. This causes many of us to end up mingling personal and business finances. This can be very problematic later, especially if business items are not clearly purchased by the business and income is not clearly transferred from the business to the individual.

If our top financial goal is to improve our financial stability then a major goal for any new business owner should be to separate their business from their own personal finances as far as possible as soon as possible. This will need to be an ongoing process.

I am always shocked to find how many older small businesses have never tried to refinance their business debt into the assets of the business. If this is not possible, they should at least make sure that all future debt is solely backed by the business. If your business fails, you want to make sure that your family doesn't lose their home. It will be hard enough to lose your business and face the financial consequences, but it can be a waking nightmare if you have huge amounts of business debt that holds your family down years after the business is gone. I can't emphasize it enough: keep your business as separate as possible from your personal finances. Better yet, start a business that doesn't require large amounts of debt to begin.

Housing

So for every rule there is an exception. Here is one. I think in many circumstances, purchasing a home with a mortgage is worth it, even though it is not a good investment. I will explain this contradiction in a moment. Hang in there. But I want to make sure to say that again: your personal residence is not an investment; it is a basic need. Stop confusing the two! Very few misguided ideas have done more to damage our financial stability during the housing bubble than the mistake of thinking about home as something other than shelter.

On its own merits, the idea that your home is an investment is quite silly. First, consider the return on your investment. Your home only appreciates at about 3 percent per year, on average. (We can all forget about the 10 percent growth of the boom years. We are paid for that with the drop in prices during the bust years.) Three percent growth is about the annual rate of inflation. So at best, you can expect that the money you put into your home will be protected from inflation, which means your home never makes any headway as an investment because any value it gains is simply canceled out by the increasing cost of the goods and services in the world around it. Next, consider that, in a typical 30 year mortgage, you are going to pay nearly double the asking price by the time you pay off your mortgage. (You do intend to pay off your mortgage, don't you?) And what about maintenance? During those thirty years, you will likely do some remodeling and pay a lot of money for it. That doesn't even count the cost of utilities and taxes.

If I came up to you and said, "I have a stock that will go up an average of 3 percent annually for the next thirty years, over the course of that thirty years you can pay twice its current face value, and every few years or so you will have to put in a few thousand dollars for maintenance and, oh, by the way, if you stop making your payments during those thirty years, I get it back," would you buy it? I hope not. Your home is not an investment; it is shelter.

The idea of your home as an investment was invented by mortgage brokers and bankers who wanted to sell us more debt based on over-inflated estimates of rising home values. It was the mortgage officer at the bank down the block, attempting to sell us a HELOC (home equity line of credit), who first convinced us to take our shelter for granted. But we wanted what he or she was selling, so we ignored that little voice in the back of our heads screaming, "Danger! Danger!" and took the plunge. Ouch!

So if owning your own home doesn't make sense from an investment point of view, why should you purchase a home? Are you better off renting? Sometimes, but not often. Owning your own home may not be a great investment, but when you compare it to renting, it offers a better mathematical return. There are some really great rent-vs.-buy calculators on the internet; don't hesitate to consult them. Just make sure they are complex enough to take into account items like maintenance and taxes.

Of course, as we have already seen, most debt calculations don't account for the risks involved with making a decision to borrow money. They only calculate the potential return you might receive if everything in your plan goes perfectly. If we are going to take our financial stability seriously, we have to account for the risk to that stability inherent in borrowing. So that again begs the question, why should we buy?

In most circumstances in which we borrow, we make a choice either between borrowing to get what we want or avoiding spending money altogether. In the case of housing, even if we do not purchase a home, we still need to pay for shelter. So the first reason to consider purchasing a home instead of renting is that, either way, you will pay for shelter either way. All things being equal, a weak investment is better than no investment—maybe.

Perhaps there is another even better way. Stop and think for a second about what the most financially stable form of shelter would be. What do you think? For my money, the paid-off home is the most stable form of shelter. Not only does a paid-for house mean that you cannot be foreclosed upon by a bank or kicked out by a landlord, but it improves your overall financial well-being because your expenses are dramatically lower compared to those neighbors who still have mortgages. Think of what it would mean to your finances to only have to pay for homeowners insurance, property taxes, and maintenance. That would change your budget, wouldn't it? Yet, we as a people take it for granted that we cannot pay off a home. We assume we cannot get there from here. That just isn't true. With focused effort it might take a decade or even two, but if we are persistent, we can pay off our home. And when we do, it will make a dramatic difference in our financial well-being.

Even if we never successfully pay off our home, a low mortgage payment itself can dramatically improve your financial stability. Once you are significantly into a mortgage, you may be able to refinance to a much lower monthly payment in an emergency. If you have large amounts of equity in your home, you could take that equity out to pay for a major emergency. Again, your home is shelter, not a piggy bank. Use your home equity only in the most desperate need, after you have already cut your other expenses to nothing. But there are times in which home equity serves as the savings of last resort.

One of the reasons many of us do not believe we can ever pay off our home is that most of us believe that we must have a thirty-year mortgage (or longer!). When you financed your last mortgage did you seriously consider a fifteen-year mortgage? Why do we all have the number "30" stuck in our head? Isn't it largely because the banks tell us that a thirty-year mortgage is better? It means we can buy more house, right? And more home means more status which is better, right? Once again, corporate marketing is keeping us from thinking for ourselves. Just remember, a thirty-year mortgage means more than double the interest for the bank compared to a fifteen-year mortgage of the same amount, and it also means a nice steady stream of profits for their stockholders. The bank is not your friend, and what they say about finances cannot be trusted.

You might be surprised by how affordable a fifteen-year mortgage can be. For example let's say you put 20 percent down on a $200,000 home and borrowed $160,000 at 4.5 percent. Your payment would be $810.70 per month and you would pay $131,850 in interest. If you chose to go with a fifteen year mortgage, you usually get a half percent break on your interest rate. At 4.0 percent on a fifteen-year mortgage, borrowing the same $160,000 you would have a monthly payment of just over 1,183.50 and pay $53,030.12 in interest, a savings of just under $80,000 in interest alone; not to mention that you will have your home paid off in half the time, dramatically lowering your risk.

The best way to see the value of a fifteen year mortgage is with a simple example. Let's say you purchased a home at 200,000 and put 20 percent down. Here is a comparison between these two situations:

	30 Year Mortgage	15 Year Mortgage	Difference:
Amount Borrowed	$160,000.00	$160,000.00	**$0.00**
Interest Rate	4.50%	4.00%	**0.50%**
Payment	$810.70	$1,183.50	**$372.80**
Interest Paid	$131,850.00	$78,819.88	**$53,030.12**
Time of Risk	30 Years	15 Years	**15 Years**

Don't get me wrong, $375 extra dollars a month is a lot to pay to take a fifteen-year mortgage. I get that, but would it be worth it to borrow a little less money and take a little less home, enabling you to pay off your mortgage in the foreseeable future rather than sometime in "la-la land?" There's a lot of risk saved when your mortgage is fifteen years shorter. If I am going to make my family's financial stability more important than status and wealth, then purchasing a home I can actually pay off just makes sense to me.

In the end, I think purchasing a home may be one of the few times borrowing makes sense, even if it is a poor investment, because you either pay a mortgage or you pay rent. However, the goal of choosing a mortgage shouldn't be to make mortgage payments for the rest of your life. Instead, you should look to try to pay off your mortgage and get to a place where no one, not a bank or a landlord, can kick you out of your home because you missed a housing payment. (Just make sure to pay your taxes or the county might come and kick you out as well.) That means, our goal must be to pay off our mortgage. To make paying off our mortgage a reasonable goal, I believe each one of us should consider purchasing less home to take a shorter mortgage.

I'm Behind on My Mortgage: Now What?

The variety of foreclosure laws in each state make it difficult to give any kind of general foreclosure advice because what may be good advice in one location may not be good advice in another. If you are facing a housing problem and need assistance, I recommend that you find a *local* Housing and Urban Development (HUD) certified housing counseling agency for advice on your local situation. HUD counseling is always free, and owners who work with counselors have a higher chance of having their mortgage modified than those who try to modify it themselves.

Homeowners want to avoid national housing counseling agencies, because they often do not know about local laws or programs. For instance, in Washington State there is a law that allows homeowners to force their lender to a mediation session at which they can present documentation showing they have the means to pay for their loan, if it were modified. These meetings help the owner stop the foreclosure process and reassure both the borrower and the state that the bank has truly evaluated all available options to help the owner stay in their home. However, national housing agencies are not eligible to refer homeowners to this mediation program; it can only be done by a Washington housing counselor or Washington attorney. Homeowners who work with national housing agencies might miss out on such opportunities. You can find a list of HUD certified housing agencies in your area by typing "HUD certified housing agency" into Google and looking for the hud.gov listing near the top of the list. I cannot emphasize enough: it is important that homeowners seeking help work with a local agency. There are all sorts of refinance options available.

Each housing problem is almost unique, so rather than trying to give advice for a wide variety of situations, I want to reemphasize something I said earlier. Homeowners should never be afraid to make a financial decision about their mortgage. You have no moral obligation to pay your mortgage. Your obligation to your bank is a contractual obligation. Your obligations to yourself and your family are moral obligations. I have seen families who destroy all of their financial well-being to keep paying their mortgage payment because they feel morally obligated to do so. This isn't right, and it isn't helpful.

I have also seen families who just cannot face up to the pain of losing their home. They scratch and claw to try to save a boat that has already sunk. Along the way, they do great financial damage to their family. They could increase their stability if they would just let go of their home, but in the moment that can be difficult to see, and it isn't always the best choice.

In the last two years I had to make those decisions myself. I was behind on my mortgage payments and in real danger of losing my home. It hurt to be in the home I love, knowing that unless something changed I would lose it. The change came last spring when my bank informed me that because my home value had risen I was now able to use one of the government assistance programs to refinance my mortgage. The good news: my payment dropped five hundred dollars per month—instant stability. The bad news: I went from a fifteen year mortgage to a forty year mortgage.

So especially in light of my advice in the last section about fifteen year mortgagesm was that a good move or bad? In the end I judged it to be a good move. Our current house payment is comparable if not lower than rents in our area. It gives us money to set aside for maintenance. Already, we've had someone out to clean the roof, take care of the dang sugar ants who had been a constant battle for years, and had our gutter repaired—avoiding a larger repair bill in the future. We're finally doing proper maintenance, something we couldn't do in the last few years. All of that makes for much lower stress and much better financial security. More importantly, if our income continues to rise, I will be able to make progress toward my paying off my student loan and saving my six month emergency fund. However, when it comes time you can bet that I will be making larger payments on my mortgage. For now, I took a giant leap toward security. Of course, if I were to start again, I would certainly be looking at a fifteen year mortgage. It's by far the better path to the ultimate in secure shelter—the paid off mortgage.

Strategy Number 2
If Possible, Live a Debt Free Life;
a.k.a. Nuclear Disarmament

I remember my encounter with this potential home buyer pretty clearly, and I don't even remember his name. I was a real estate agent at the time, and I didn't get the sale. I don't even remember how I ended up meeting the guy. What I remember distinctly is that he was probably the wealthiest person I had ever met up to that point. He had homes all over the place, California, Hawaii and elsewhere. He was in land development, among other things. He wanted to buy a home in my area as a place where his assistant could work. He wasn't interested in living there. He just wanted a good investment. The year was 2007 and the housing market was weakening. He was looking to score a deal off a distressed builder with a high-end property that he couldn't sell. We were looking at homes just under $1,000,000; he was paying cash.

We were riding in his vehicle, a late 1980s or early 1990s Honda Accord. He was driving. (He liked to be in control.) For those of you who don't remember, these cars were known for their longevity and low maintenance costs. Here was a wealthy man with an eye for value.

Not much else sticks out in my mind except one thing he said. He and his assistant were discussing how it would be convenient to put the money he intended to use for development at one of our local banks because it had branches in my area as well as in Eugene, Oregon, where he had other business interests.

I knew something about the bank. In our area they had a reputation as one of the two most accommodating lenders for builders. They offered creative lending products for land development.

Wanting to appear knowledgeable, I piped up from the back seat and said something about how helpful this bank was to property developers, and how they had all sorts of creative lending products. I can still see his eyes in the rear view mirror as they gave me a look that said that I didn't get it. "I don't ever borrow money," he said. "I only lend it." I think I lost the deal right at that moment.

That encounter with wealth has always stuck with me. I learned two things that day. First, the truly wealthy don't always or even often flaunt it. We are used to seeing the percentage of the wealthy who seek fame: sports heroes, rock stars, actors, morally questionable debutant queens and the like. But most of the wealthy I have met are very different than this media image. They aren't like Donald Trump, eating gold-plated caviar off diamond-encrusted plates. This kind of conspicuous consumption is more often a sign of financial brittleness than it is of true financial stability. Did you know that Donald Trump almost went personally bankrupt and has sold off major portions of his hotels to pay off debts? I wonder if we would even still talk about him if NBC hadn't saved his sorry butt with a TV show.

The truly wealthy don't often pursue status. They don't need to. They have already made it. The pursuit of Rolex watches and $100,000 vehicles is for wannabes like you and me. Why pursue status when you've already achieved it?

More importantly, I learned the truly wealthy don't often borrow money, although they may lend it to others. Then they sit back and transfer the wealth from the fool's pocket to their own.

So which do you want to be? Do you want to be the person who gives his money away to others? Or do you want to live a debt-free life? The choice is up to you, but if you value your financial stability, it is time to take the nukes out of your wallet and make it a goal to never borrow money for anything ever again. It might not be a goal you can meet, you might borrow to pay for college, buy a business, purchase a home, or when in desperate need, but you will surely have better financial stability if you try. Any other method of personal finance makes your odds of success a lot longer, and we have already seen how bad we can be at calculating risk.

Chapter 9:
A Financial Road Map

In our section on financial strategies, I've argued that financial stability isn't so much about how much income you make or whether or not you can afford to take a vacation every summer. At times, you may pursue financial stability with all your might and still take steps backward. Financial stability comes much more from doing the best with what you have.

Pursuing financial stability isn't a hindrance toward building wealth either. On the contrary, by taking care of first things first you are much more likely than your neighbor to build permanent or semi-permanent wealth, who pursues a wealthy lifestyle right out of the gate. A wealthy lifestyle without savings is like a house of cards balanced on the head of a pin.

So what should we do with our money when we have something left over after we have purchased our food, clothing, shelter, transportation, emergency savings, and paid all the rest of the bills? Without a plan for our extra money, it is likely to be blown on consumer goods without protecting our stability in the future. This will just lead to trouble down the road. We need a financial road map, a life-long strategic plan that can provide a compass-point toward which we march. We need a path toward stability.

The basics of this plan come from Dave Ramsey. I've already mentioned that I respect Ramsey's work. His principles are right. Yet he still tends to think like someone who always has a surplus; for instance, on his monthly budget form he places both charitable giving and savings above food, clothing, and shelter. I disagree here. In truth, your basic needs come before savings or giving. If I differ from him, it is because I write as someone who has worked hard but isn't wealthy. Those of you who are familiar with his work will recognize these as his baby steps. I've adjusted them to reflect the differences in the way I think.

Step 0: On a monthly basis, make sure you are not spending more than you earn *(Make sure your boat is not leaking.)*

Step 1: Secure your basic needs: food, clothing, and shelter

Step 2: Create a $1,000 emergency fund *(Keep this money in a cash based account such as a money market fund or savings account.)*

Step 3: Pay off all debts as fast as possible, other than your home *(This includes student loans, medical bills, and credit cards.)*

Step 4: Increase your emergency fund to six to ten months of your basic needs

Step 5: Begin saving 15% of your income for retirement

Step 6: If so desired, save for your child's college education

Step 7: Pay off your mortgage early

Step 8: Express your values with your money *(You have taken care of your responsibilities; now be who you were meant to be.)*

One of the tricks to using this plan is to recognize that you will go back and forth between the steps many times over the course of your life. For instance, let's say that you have built your $1,000 emergency fund and then have begun to hammer away at your debt. It feels great to be making progress, doesn't it? But then a car repair suddenly takes your $1,000 and cuts it down to $200. You then need to move backwards from step three to step two and replenish your emergency fund before you pay anything more than the minimum required on your credit card debt. In our new economic reality there will be many families, like my own, who will bounce back and forth between steps zero through three of this plan. It may take years to get to step four.

This same back-and-forth may continue for much of your life. You may be toward the end of paying off your mortgage early and be suddenly laid off. You quickly trim the budget and, for the next several months, you look hard for work. To cover your now reduced monthly expenses, you work through about half your emergency savings when you add it to your unemployment. So what happens when you finally take that new job with more responsibility but at 70% of the salary you had before? (Pay cuts, just another wonderful benefit of our new economic reality!) The simple answer is to look at where you are on the steps of the road map and move back to the step that is not longer completed, complete it once again, and move forward. In many cases, this would mean placing retirement spending on hold, and telling your teenager he gets to consider studying harder for scholarships or to go to community college while you work to bring your emergency fund back up to full strength.

I have found no better road map to bring financial stability to a household. It is simple, clear, and precise, but it isn't the end-all and be-all of financial thinking, either. Perhaps you could do better, or you like a different plan. As long as your strategic plan supports the mission to create financial stability, that's all good. By far the most important point in this section is to have a plan. If you do not have a plan for your surplus income, you may soon find yourself with wonderful new furniture but no home to put it in.

Families who use these eight steps as their financial road map have a great shot at making strides toward financial stability. However, unless they commit to avoiding the use of debt in all but the most dire of personal circumstances, their efforts are in vain. Debt undermines all efforts to increase our financial stability. A plan is also only as good as its implementation. For that we need to look at the specific tactics we can use to spend our money based on our best interests.

Strategy Number 3
Follow a Financial Road Map

Sometimes to fix a problem, you have to do a little cleaning first. You have to recognize that the way you did things before didn't work. It is time to clear your head. All the stratagems, schemes, and plans you have used to get by need to be put aside so you can put something new in their place. Consider this a chance to clear off a desktop buried under all these failed attempts to feel better financially and find the hard surface underneath it all.

Take a moment and just sweep all those plans and dreams onto the floor. Clean off your mental desk. Don't worry; just because your plans are on the floor doesn't mean you won't be able to accomplish them. In fact, sometimes by taking a step sideways you might be able to accomplish them much faster than you hope. Do you have a clean surface to work with? Good. It's time to get back to financial basics. The money you make is the money you spend on a monthly basis. Spend it on meeting your immediate needs first. Then use your surplus to secure your basic needs in the future. It is that simple. A financial road map is a vital tool to keeping us on track over the long term. Here is the irony: the more dedicated you become to taking care of first things first, the more money you will have left over each month to do the things you want to do, including all those plans you just swept onto the floor.

Tactics

Chapter 10:
It's Alive! It's Alive!

In the first section of our book, we adopted a new coherent and feasible financial mission: we seek to secure our basic needs, both now and in the future, and to do nothing that would harm our ability to secure them on an ongoing basis. In the second section of our book, we looked at three strategies necessary to accomplish this mission:

1. Live below our income and save the extra for a rainy day.
2. Seek to live in a debt-free manner.
3. Follow a financial road map.

In the final section of our book, we need to take this mission along with our strategies and turn them into something real. We need to adopt day-to-day activities that help us accomplish our goals and live out our mission. We need healthy financial tactics.

If we are not living out our mission with our money, it isn't because the tactics we need aren't available. In fact, I think most financial advice within the United States falls into the tactics category. There are whole magazines devoted to determining which washer, stock, car, or loan product you should purchase. Just a cursory search of the internet will reveal five tips for any financial problem and twenty quick and easy ways to generate wealth or save money. The media culture of the United States treats personal finance like any other consumer product, generating reams of advice to scratch the latest consumer itch. Very few advice columns think strategically, and it takes going to the editorial page of your local newspaper to find anything that questions the consumer-spending driven mission of the United States. Most of these editorial columns are politically driven and give at best a mixed financial message.

Not that I think such tactical advice is bad. Tactical activities provide a key component of a healthy financial plan. Yet, way back in the first chapter when I introduced the idea of mission, strategy, and tactics, I argued when the mission or the strategy becomes confused, military planners tended to default toward the easiest piece to control: the tactics.

This is what I see happening to financial advice in the United States. As a country, we haven't defined a sustainable financial mission. As a result, our strategies haven't made sense or have been nonexistent. In the end, we have exalted tactics to the place of strategy and mission. Thus we have a glut of tactical products on the market, from Mint.com and Quicken to *Consumer Reports* and *Forbes*. All of it attempting to teach us how to be a wise day-to-day consumer but failing to provide a coherent way to make sense of what is often contradictory advice. Many consumers have just shut down, preferring to ignore all advice rather than listen to advice that seems to contradict what they heard yesterday. On the one hand, we have a glut of financial advice, while on the other, we starve for clear information.

There is no need to reinvent the wheel, so we will not re-cover the well-trodden ground of how to find the best appliances or avoid scams. If you are looking to hone your financial thinking in this way, which you should be, *Consumer Reports* provides an excellent resource to teach you to cost compare. Or take a look at any of the books by Clark Howard, an excellent thinker and trainer in this area.

Bringing the Monster to Life

Rather than just trying to improve your overall spending savvy, our book will look at tactics in a slightly different fashion. (Be warned, in a book full of bad, stretched, and barely plausible metaphors, what follows is possibly the worst.) What we have right now is a monster lying on the table, waiting to be brought to life. We have our clear mission and the strategies necessary to get there. We also have more articles, blogs ,and books than we will ever need, to help us make the right decisions on a day-to-day basis. The capacitors are full of energy. Somehow we need some kind of switch that will channel all that energy into the monster and get it moving in the right direction. (See—I warned you about the metaphor.)

If we are going to accomplish our goals then our tactics must help us make sure that our resources go to the three strategies we outlined in the last section of our book and we don't get diverted to other things. But just how much food, clothing, shelter, transportation, and savings is needed? When can we start spending money beyond our basic necessities? How much savings is enough? If we are going to fulfill our mission, we need to know how to answer these questions. We need tactics that will help us see when we are achieving our goals. We also need them to give us feedback along the way, to let us know whether or not we are meeting our goals and to get us back on track before we get far off course.

Dare I say we need a plan? We already have a financial road map that helps set some concrete long-term goals for our money. However, that strategic plan won't tell me whether or not I can afford steak every night or if I need to look for the ground round at $1.99 a pound. To make that kind of decision, we need something much more concrete and short-term: we need a monthly budget.

There, I said it, the financial equivalent of the "F" word. However, before you throw your e-reader across the room in disgust, or after you picked it back up if you already had done so, let me just say the problem with most budgets is they are completely worthless.

I promise, I am not going to tell you how much you *should* spend on anything. In fact, one of the major problems with most budgets is they don't reflect your values. Most often, budgets feel like your mother looking over your shoulder telling you to be sensible and buy that ugly dress instead of this better one because that ugly thing is cheaper. No wonder budgets don't work. *This* budget you get to make completely your own. No mothers allowed; unless you want to include her. This is where you get to shine the most. Your personal budget is the fingerprint that you place on your own personal finances. It is the place where you get to tell your money what you want it to do for you. It is your act of financial individuality. Chapter 10 will discuss budgeting in detail.

Mothers may be easily dismissed, but spouses and significant others aren't so easily gotten rid of. If you have joint finances, I have already argued you will be much better off if you find some way to agree on what the joint priorities will be for your money. Here is where the rubber meets the road. Life will be much easier for you if you create one plan, particularly when you see the kind of plan we intend to create. It will be very important that both of you buy into that plan. You might as well forget about announcing just how it will be to your spouse because they have the power to blow up your plan at every turn. This will require a willingness to negotiate and either find common ground or find some kind of compromise that both of you can live with. Having said that, I have seen very successful relationships in which both parties keep their finances separate from the other because they had different goals. That is also an option.

Yet all the planning in the world won't matter one bit if we don't *follow* the plan. Isn't that what usually happens with our efforts to put together a budget? We put together an awesome plan, and then next week we blow it, kinda sorta on purpose. Or it doesn't actually match our needs, and so the whole thing just doesn't work, and the house of cards falls to pieces. Chapter 11 will cover how to spend money in such a way that it follows your plan and how to know in an instant if your plan isn't working. It will also make clear how to adjust the plan with one easy step.

Write a List of Your Current Values

Before we get started budgeting, we need to do a little preparatory work first. Do you remember way back in Chapter Three, when I said how you actually spend your money is a statement of your values? Well, before we can direct our income toward our necessities, we need to do a little work to find out just what goods and services we currently value. If we are going to make a budget that is yours and yours alone, we will need to get some idea of your expenses on a monthly basis. Here is the good news; if you do this well the first time, you shouldn't have to do it again. Once you get your budgeting system rolling, it will be just a matter of tweaking it based upon your current circumstances.

Most often I found my clients knew their regular bills on a monthly basis. Since they paid them monthly, they understood what their cable bill or water bill usually cost them. In fact, when I say the word budget, many people think all I mean are their monthly bills. They imagine the rest of their money as a big pile from which everything else is taken as needed. They often have no idea how much is spent on food, gasoline, eating out, or coffee. However, this thinking can cause all sorts of problems if it is allowed to continue, because that pile of cash includes payments for luxury items as well as for basic necessities, such as food and transportation. These necessities can easily be threatened by spending on unnecessary items.

I once counseled a graduate student in architecture with a wife and a young baby. They lived on a very tight income. After adding up his debit-card purchases, he found he was spending around $140 per month on coffee. He had no idea he was seriously threatening his family's well-being through his coffee habit.

Like the young architect, most of us use some form of plastic money for these kinds of purchases, and while it is a habit I want you to break, for now it is a bit lucky for us because individual debit-card purchases and credit-card purchases are much easier to track. That makes it quite possible to find out how you have spent your money in the last month.

If you spend cash, first of all, congratulations! You are way ahead of the game. However, it will make it more difficult for you to determine just what you purchased with that money.

If you have receipts, you will do better. If you don't have receipts try to remember how much money you put in your wallet or purse over the last month and then try to account for where most, if not all, went.

Please don't lose perspective about this whole exercise. The goal here isn't to track our expenses down to the penny. Rather, I want you to know that you spend between $250 and $300 per month on gasoline, and that your bill for eating out was about $200 last month. So find the most recent copy of your bank statements and credit card statements, or go online and download them. If you use cash, find your receipts or make a list of all your cash purchases. Then take each item you purchased and categorize it for yourself. You get to make the categories; I don't make them for you. Now even though you get to make your own categories, how you set them up will determine what kind of control and feedback you get throughout the month on your spending. So, I would suggest you try to be specific about your needs vs. wants. For instance, many people include personal products such as makeup, hair care, and soap, as well as household products such as paper towels and napkins in the same category as groceries. My wife and I personally don't do this, because we are much more willing to compromise on what we spend for personal and household items than we are on how much money we spend on food. If I have to wipe up spilled milk with a kitchen towel for a week instead of paper towel while I wait for the new budget, I would rather do that than not be able to afford the milk for my daughter to spill. Make sure optional items such as cable, and entertainment expenses, are kept far away from your needs. No need to have your reality TV habit threatening your light bill; not all utilities have equal weight.

If you need help getting started on a list of personal expense categories, you can find them all over the internet. It might be a good idea to take a look at them to make sure that your personal categories are not too specific or too broad. There is a bit of a Goldilocks zone here. Dave Ramsey's five-page budget form provides a helpful list. You can search for it on the internet. Quicken's list of personal expense categories works very well. If neither of these are enough, try your favorite search engine. I like some of the Google Docs personal finance templates. They have pretty clear lists of expense categories. You might find them useful as well.

Make sure you are honest about what you spent last month. Some of us will recognize, last month might have been a little bit different than the average month. You might have had three weddings to attend, or you might have had your in-laws in town for a week and you ended up eating out a bunch. This might make you object that last month shouldn't count and you shouldn't do this project until you have a typical month. Here's a little secret. No month is average, and no budget should be based on averages either.

I will explain that more in the next chapter. For now, just don't fret about what you spent last month that seems out of the ordinary; just write it all down and get it categorized. You will need to do this at some point, and remember, no one is telling you what you will spend next month. If last month was weird, when we budget you will simply adjust your budget for next month to account for the weirdness. I promise you are in control here, so there is no harm in looking at the truth.

However, be warned, some of you are not going to like what you see. Remember, self-judgment is the enemy of change, so work on just accepting the reality of your choices. I hope this exercise leads you to make healthy changes in your expenses. It may lead you to realize you have been prioritizing status over stability. Again, all your spending is your choice; if you want to put a $1,200 pair of Manolo leather boots in your budget every month and skip the rent payment, go for it. What is your plan when you end up sleeping in your car and 25 percent of your income is being garnished by your creditors? If you value stability over status, now is the time to start making changes and to direct your income toward your necessities instead of status items. We are all on that journey with you.

Add and Subtract to Reflect Your Current Values

Before we move along, I need to make a quick comment to those of you in relationships in which you intermingle your money. So far what you have done has been mostly fact-based. You simply added up and categorized your expenses for the last month. I hope both of you were able to reserve judgment on your significant other. Most often, it is easier to see where the other person is threatening your financial stability than it is to see where you are threatening theirs. From here until the end of the chapter, we are going to move into a couple of exercises that are much more based in opinion than they are in fact. They are value-driven, and differences in values are a tremendous source of tension in relationships.

So I would strongly recommend you do the next couple of exercises separately. (I'll tell you when to start working together again.) Don't debate any choices or any decisions your spouse has made until the end of the chapter. Once you have finished, you put your two plans together, and come up with the categories and values for the household. That will be the time to bring out all your compromise and negotiating skills. For now, just work on expressing, in as nondivisive a way as possible, your own personal financial values. Ready? Good.

Take a slow minute and ask yourself a couple of questions: Are there any expenses missing from this list that I currently value? And are there things that we used to value but we no longer value that we might remove from our list? This is where you get to express your current values, which I hope now reflect a better sense of urgency when it comes to your basic needs. After seeing what you spent your money on last month, you get to add those categories of items you now want to spend money on next month. (Hint: This is where you would add emergency savings to the list if you do not have any.)

Rank Your List

Once you complete your personal list of expense categories, you will have a much better sense of what you personally value at this moment in time. If you are willing to be honest, you will also have revealed some areas where you could use a little improvement. Now is when you get to change the way you think about certain items. Our economy does not guarantee financial well-being to every hard-working individual. This means, we must make sure to guide our money toward those goods and services that support our needs before we spend them on other items. This must cause us to place certain categories higher on the list than other categories. So not all of the categories we spent money on last month have equal value and weight.

It is time to rank our expense categories in order of importance to us. So go ahead and rewrite your list of expense categories, not in order of amount but rather in order of importance. Place the most important expenses at the top of the page.

You already know my opinions on this matter; you must take care of your basic needs before you spend money on other items. Food, clothing, shelter, and all the items you need to have to provide your family with those three items should come first. That means right behind the big three should come items like transportation, your *necessary* utilities, and items like medical expenses. Next, we need to make sure we have at least a baby emergency fund of $1,000. Or if we already have that, we need to fund our other savings priorities, such as our full emergency fund, a new car, or our retirement. This takes care of your immediate necessities and your long term necessities.

Before we move forward with categories beyond our basic needs, let's take a step back, and look at the remaining categories of expenses. What is left that isn't on the list? A lot, right? There are probably some items that are very important to you sitting on the table. There are also other bills, such as your credit card expenses, which are not necessary for your survival but are important because they threaten your financial future. So what order will you put these in? At this point, I am slightly less opinionated. Debt, in all forms, represents a serious threat to your long-term financial stability, so eliminating debt needs to be a high priority after your basic needs have been met. However, once you have taken care of your immediate needs there are other items to be considered as well. Cello lessons, soccer, and other kid expenses are high priorities for me. Those duties to my family matter much, and as long as I am paying much more than my minimums, I might choose to pay a little less than I could toward my debts to keep those kid investments in place. Once again, hard and fast rules here are difficult.

Yet, if you never make sacrifices to get out of debt you probably never will live a financially stable life. Way too many of us fall into the trap of, "Well, Susie needed that new Disney princess play house for her birthday, so I had to use the credit card." If you are still stuck on that path, you won't ever find financial stability.

So now you have a general idea of your expenses for the last month. (Perhaps we are a little embarrassed by the list.) We have rewritten our list of expenses in priority order, and we have made sure that list includes all expenses we would like to add to our spending to improve our financial security. There really isn't anything left to do other than create our budget. That is what we will do in the next chapter.

Ahem... Between this chapter and the next is where those of you in relationships have to do the hard work of reconciling your separate lists. Remember this isn't about winning everything you want. It's about being a team together, so negotiate in good faith. But don't be afraid to stand up for what is right. Your financial stability is worth insisting upon. Don't let your spouse's love of cars, clothing, electronics, or cosmetics threaten your shelter or food supply. If you are the spouse who has been caught with your hand in the consumer cookie jar, please don't feel ashamed. You are no different from the rest of us. I have been there. In my family, I am the spender, and I break the budget. Just be humble, and take it as an opportunity to grow personally and become a more generous person. No one dies and puts on their tombstone: I owned a great car. But many would love to have their children write: He cared for us.

Chapter 11:
Zero-Balance What?

So what do you think when you hear the word budget? Most of us think of some outside force, like a parent, trying to tell us what to do. We see budgets as ineffective stodgy tools that have little to do with the way we spend and use money on a day-to-day basis. I cannot say I disagree with these assessments. Most budgets are just these things.

For instance, the most common form of budget would be what I call the "look-back" budget, which works by averaging out what you have spent on different categories of goods and services for the last few months or, more often, the last year. The household then tries to keep expenses to these averages each month going forward. This is the type of budget Quicken or Mint.com will help you create. What a complete waste of time! The makers of Quicken, Intuit, really should be smarter than that. They are too good at creating useful financial software not to know better. Perhaps they are more interested in getting you to purchase their credit card and all their other product tie-ins than they are in helping you financially? Maybe, they are a corporation after all. Their job is to take your money.

There are several reasons this type of budget will not work. First of all, a look-back budget does not account for any price changes in the future. For instance, if the average price of gasoline was $2.75 per gallon when I created my budget and now it costs $4.15, my average expenditure on gasoline will be way off. How is my family supposed to live on that past number? Look-back budgets fall down like a house of cards whenever a category doesn't match what happened in the past.

This points out another weakness of look-back budgets: what happens when you run into a month that isn't average? Months with unusual expenses happen with obnoxious regularity. In fact, the truly unusual month is the month in which our expenses will match our averages for the last year. For instance, tires wear out on a regular but occasional basis. I doubt my $50 monthly allowance for car repairs will allow me to purchase four new tires, and most likely I have not saved the extra car repair money each month left over after my oil change and kept it for the long term expense of tires. So now what do I do? I know what to do; I will get out my Quicken credit card and incorporate the payments into my budget because they are easy to average each month. What do you think of that idea? What a great way to make Quicken profitable and bankrupt my children!

Next, just how much do I have available to spend on eating out? Look-back budgets do not take income into consideration. As we have seen, our first financial priority as a household is to make sure our expenses are not greater than our income on a monthly basis. What if we had been spending more than we made each of the last 12 months? Our look-back budget would average out these expenses and tell us to just go right ahead and continue to spend what we spent last year, leading us right down the path to bankruptcy. Or what would happen if I got a promotion at work? I may be able to save more than I did last month and take my family out to eat once in a while. A look-back budget will keep telling us to spend the same amount that we used to spend for a category such as eating out or savings.

With a look back budget, we end up in an antagonistic relationship to the budget on the page. I used to feel that way all the time. It wasn't that long ago, I felt like my budget was the authority figure telling me what to do instead of my tool to direct my spending in the future. What happens if my values change? What if I now decide I value an emergency fund more than eating out? My look-back budget tells me to keep putting money aside for eating out, even though I now realize I need an emergency fund first.

Such budgets are a complete waste of time if we want our budget to direct our spending toward financial stability and away from status. It doesn't provide us with either a path to such a goal or with the correct feedback we need to see when and where we need to change course to stay on target. We will have to find a different way to budget.

Look Forward Not Backward

A healthy budget should begin by examining our past expenses, whether it be one month like we did in the last chapter or twelve months like Quicken, but that is only the very first step. Looking back provides a clear picture of our current values. However, looking back is a terrible way to make decisions regarding how to spend (or invest) your money in the future. (Stock and mutual fund investors, take note.) A healthy budget should look forward, with humility, and try to anticipate what expenses are about to come our way. Then we should allocate resources to meet those needs.

No one knows all of the future. But financially, much of it can be predicted. For instance, Christmas arrives every year on December 25th, and in most families it has a huge financial impact. Perhaps looking ahead could help keep that impact from being so damaging to our financial health. Tires mysteriously wear out. Retirement does eventually come for us all. If we spend our time looking into the past, we will not prepare properly for such events. On the other hand, if we have consistently looked forward into the future, we will be much closer to covering our long-term needs than otherwise.

So budgets should be based on what we want our money to do for us in the future, not based on what happened in the past. By looking to the future they also can account for changes in our income and expenses. If my income increases and my budget is about the future, then I will account for what I am going to do with that money in the future. If gasoline suddenly jumps to $5.00 per gallon and if I am looking ahead, I will account for the change in gasoline prices and change my expenses accordingly.

Looking ahead when you budget also makes the budget your own. If yesterday I valued lattes over an emergency fund, I am in no way bound to that choice if my budget is looking to the future. I am free to change my values any time I please, and those changes can be reflected in my budget.

Despite all these benefits, I think there is one obvious reason most people base their budgets on past averages. A budget based on past averages appears to require little work or maintenance. I can adjust my budget once a year, avoid "wasting" any more time on it and go back to my status-driven life. On the other hand, a budget based on predicting future expenses cannot be done once a year. How often you budget really depends upon you, but I would advise that you budget for the future at least once a month, perhaps more often if it works better with your household's paychecks. For the purposes of our discussion, we will assume you will budget your money on a monthly basis.

Many people believe if they make financial decisions based upon average expenditures from the past, they won't have to think so hard or make so many decisions. Is that truly the case? What about all the decisions you need to make just to keep your house of cards together? What about all the unexpected and abnormal expenses you have not accounted for in your average budget? Each one of those "emergencies" requires decisions and energy to manage the crisis, and this is a recipe for stress and anxiety. The energy used to manage this unnecessary financial stress far outweighs the conveniences of look-back thinking. Isn't that so often the case? That which we do for the sake of convenience often ends up costing us much more time and energy than it saves.

It is true that a budgeting process committed to the future does require monthly maintenance, but the time spent creating a spending plan each month is much less than the time it takes to put out the fires caused by traditional look-back budgeting, and it is much less stressful. Truly, at this point, my wife and I can get through a budget and pay our bills in one to two hours a month, but our budget is quite simple. If we had a more typical financial situation, it might take us three hours. That is one Saturday morning a month at the worst. Besides, budgeting without taking into account future changes in expenses does not seem to me to jibe well with our stated mission of creating financial stability.

No matter how we create our budget, the future is quite impossible to fully predict. At best, our budget will be an estimate of expenses and it must account for the unknown. Thus, we must approach the future with humility when we budget and leave margin for both human error and unexpected events.

Looking forward each time we plan can help us make sure we remember to account for the unknown when we spend our money.

Budget Every Dollar

Remember how I mentioned most of us have our budget and then the pile of money left over (or not) from which we take everything else? I think we continue to budget this way because we have an antagonistic relationship with our budget. Rather than it being our tool, we instead see it as someone else's way of badgering us into being upstanding responsible people. Yuck! So the budget gets that money over there, and this pile of money left over is mine to do with as I please.

It's time to take back a sense of ownership over your money. Your money isn't forcing you to do anything. You get to make all the choices when it comes to your money. How you spend your money is simply an expression of your values. So express yourself. Just be honest about what you value, and be willing to take responsibility for your choices. With this attitude you can end the "theirs and mine" thinking when it comes to *your* money. You earned it. It is all your money.

Now, money is both precious and slippery. If you let your materialistic desires control how you use your money, you will soon find yourself with a kick-butt car... *payment* and no place to live. I assume you value your necessities above other things. Now that all the money you earn is yours again, make sure you don't forget it.

I think we can agree the pile-o'-money plan is a very wasteful way to use money. Any whim that comes into our head is likely to get acted upon. We simply check the bank account, do some quickie math in our head regarding what bills will come out before we get paid on Friday, and then throw that high end food processor, new game system, and sofa/love seat combination voucher tag into our basket, and proceed to check out. Then, after everything has been purchased, we have our Homer Simpson moment and realize we forgot about the electric bill while we were doing our quickie math. Have you ever tried to return a sofa and love seat combo? Awkward!

If we want our money to express our values, the pile-o'-money budget has to go. Every dollar we earn must be included in our budget; we don't have any money to waste. But what exactly do I mean by the word "waste"? Some of you are already assuming that I am now going to go back on my promise and start telling you how to spend your money. Not so fast; I will simply say we waste money when we use it for items that do not reflect our desired values. So if I value food more than I value a new love seat, I would have wasted my money if I cannot eat because I purchased a love seat instead of food. On the other hand, if my latte habit is important to me, and I have taken care of my needs, put away a large sum toward my emergency savings and paid for those items I value more than lattes, then allocating resources to my latte habit isn't wrong. In fact, I would argue you would be wasting money if you *didn't* allocate money for lattes. They are important to you, right?

The trick is to make sure your latte habit doesn't threaten your light bill or anything else you value more than lattes. To do this, you have to do three different things when you budget. First, you need to make sure that there is an appropriate category in your budget for lattes. (You did do that, right? You really did include all the things you value when you wrote your categories, right?) For me, I use the category of "pocket money" to cover these types of items. I value going out to breakfast once in a while, and I used to have rotary dues to pay, etc. These expenses need to be funded but controlled, because it is the money that is frittered away that can do the most damage to a budget. Remember the student who was spending $140 on coffee every month? He didn't give up on buying coffee every month. Instead, he put two $20s in his wallet each month and limited himself to that amount until pay day. Coffee was valuable to him but not more valuable than his family.

Next, make sure everything you spend is included in the same budget—no more little piles of money here and separate mini-budgets there. If it comes from your income for the month then you need to include it in your budgets.

Finally, and this should be clear by now, you need to make sure you allocate every dollar you earn when you budget. If you don't want your money wasted, you need to tell every dollar what you want it to do. Remember, money that is spent on items you do not value is money wasted, plain and simple. Make sure you are telling your money what to do and not the other way around.

Zero-Balance Budgeting

So what we need is a budgeting system that looks forward to the future, allows us to express our values, allocates every dollar, and guides us toward financial stability. That's a bit of a tall order, don't you think? Well, my proprietary software is up to the task, and if you will simply mail me three payments of $99.99, I will happily send you the software package that will make it happen.... Actually, my solution is really quite elegant and simple. Are you ready? Let's do it.

Start with a blank piece of lined paper, or if you are a computer person like me, start with a blank spreadsheet. (A spreadsheet might be a little easier, because you may end up adding things in the middle later.) Now take that list of expense categories you created to reflect your values in the last chapter and write them on your blank paper in priority order. At the top should be your three necessities: food, clothing, and shelter. Then work your way down. If you are working with someone else on joint finances, you need to look at your joint priorities, which you negotiated at the end of the last chapter. (I hope you were able to come to agreement. If you haven't, now is the time to get it done.) Don't yet fill in any amounts next to them; for now we are interested in generating a list of categories in order.

The list you just created could be considered your master list. You might want to make a quick copy of it or save the document as your master copy before we continue, because it will make budgeting in future months easier when you have a list of commonly used categories already created. On the other hand, once you get the hang of this, many of your categories will stay the same, so I find it easier to just open last month's spreadsheet and look and then save it to this month before I begin. This allows me to refer back to what we spent last month for gasoline, etc., and adjust the numbers accordingly. This is helpful for planning, even if prices have changed.

The next step is to add anything to that list that will happen this month and hasn't yet made the list. So if the month is June, and you have two weddings and three college graduation parties to attend, then you need to make sure that all of those gifts are included in the budget. It won't do you any good to budget for last month. You need to get all the expenses for this month included on the paper. Don't forget categories like pocket money, Netflix, app store games, and all those other expenses that usually aren't included. Remember, we are budgeting for every dollar we earn, so those legitimate categories have to be included in the budget. Did you include everything? I bet not, but for now let's assume you did. There will be time to go back later and add things you missed. At the bottom of your list make sure to add a line called "grease" or perhaps you could call it "humility." This will be the amount you leave in the budget to cover your mistakes, like forgetting that you have to pay for school pictures or your best friend's bridal shower (I hope you didn't forget that!).

Now leave a few blank lines. (This is for the other things you have forgotten to add.) Then write in the word "Income" on your paper or spreadsheet. Now you will need to calculate your income for the coming month and write it on the sheet next to the word. For most of you this will be relatively easy. Just get out your last couple of pay stubs and figure out what you can count on bringing home this month. We are not interested in your gross pay right now. We want to know the amount of money you have available to spend on paying for your monthly expenses, so we want the actual amount you will bring home.

Be careful if you include overtime. You will be using every dollar that you write on the page, so make sure to be conservative with your income. Better to be pleasantly surprised rather than find yourself in yet another financial bind because you overestimated your income. Companies have a habit of suddenly cutting off overtime, so if possible it is best to leave that amount aside for now. If you earn extra money during the month, you can always use it to increase your emergency savings, pay off debt or move your financial stability forward in some other way.

For those of you on commission or other more variable forms of income, you are going to need to make an estimate here. Again, the trick for you is to be very conservative on your income. This will be hard for some of us sales people. We like to anticipate big things, but in this case it can really hurt you down the road if you were living a six figure life and end up with a mid or low five-figure income. So be humble and conservative when you estimate your income. Once you have a figure in mind, write it down on the sheet. (It is important for us to write down our income before we fill amounts in our expense categories, otherwise those of us with variable incomes might be tempted to design an income to fit our expenses.)

Now it is time to fill in your anticipated expenses for the next month. Next to each category write down the amount of money you think you will need to spend before your next budget begins. That includes every category where you believe you will spend money next month, including workout videos, pedicures, and online game subscriptions. Here is where your work adding up your expenses from last month will be very helpful. For many categories what you spent last month will be a good guide to what you will spend this month. However, if you plan to take an extra trip with the vehicle this month, make sure to account for that when you figure your gas budget. Here again is an opportunity to let your values shine and hopefully to increase your financial stability by funding those categories that help and remove funding from categories that undermine your stability.

There are a couple of categories you must fund each month; they are especially important when you begin this process. If you are used to spending pocket money, if at all possible try to fund that category. Be reasonable with yourself, too. If you have spent $250 per month on pocket money items, don't expect to get to $40 overnight. On the other hand, if you don't have the money to spare, you might just have to look at your values and take the credit cards out of your wallet so you can't be tempted. (Haven't you cut those things up yet?)

Next, and this is much more important than anything else you do, you must generously fund the "humility" category. You will always need to leave some margin for error in your budget, but this is especially important until you get the hang of this budgeting system. You will screw this up, so make sure you have left something to cover those mistakes. If we are going make this budgeting system work, it won't help to have it send us sideways out of the gate, so I cannot emphasize this enough. Fund your "humility" category. You will use it.

Once you have figured out your desired expenses in each category for the next month, write the words "Monthly Expenses" directly below the word "Income." Now add up your expenses and simply subtract them from your anticipated income. So what happened? I will predict one of two things happened. First, you have huge amounts of money left over, which leaves you scratching your head because you never feel like you have money left over. In this case, I challenge you to go back and look at your expenses and be more honest about what you spend on a monthly basis. If you double-, triple-, and quadruple-check and you still have extra money (I wish), then use that extra money to increase your stability by saving an emergency fund or paying off debt once you have $1,000 in the bank.

The much more likely possibility is that your eyeballs are bigger than your income and you are planning to spend more this month than you brought home. In this case, it is time to make some choices. It is time to trim your expenses. Why? Because our first strategy for increasing our financial stability is to make sure that we do not spend more than we take in on a monthly basis. We have to keep our boat floating. Any month in which our expenses are greater than our income, we must cut the budget until they are equal. (Remember, savings and "humility" are already included in your list of expenses, so you do not need to worry about your budget balancing on the head of a pin; your margin is already included in the budget.) When you get your budget to balance, write a zero on your budget form underneath your total expense number, which should now exactly equal the income number written above it. You have now completed your first zero-balance budget.

Zero-Balance Budgeting Is Sexy

So how long did it take you to get this little project done? The first time my wife and I tried to do this, it must have taken eight hours, and within a week we were back at the drawing board to try again. Don't be surprised if you have to spend some time redoing what you just finished this week. Don't give up; it does get better. Usually on about the third try your budget suddenly clicks and takes much less time. This month my budget took just a couple of hours to plan and execute, including paying all my bills. Healthy money management requires learning and practice. Hang in there; we all fell and scraped our knees the first time we did this.

However, stop and take a moment to think about what you have just done. In one fell swoop we have created a plan that, if followed, will automatically make sure we do not spend more than we bring in. We have focused all our resources on meeting our needs first, and we know exactly what luxury items we can afford and what we cannot afford. Our values ruled the day and money now serves us, not the other way round. I haven't found any other way to budget that is as focused and empowering. At the beginning of the previous section, I said we needed a budgeting system that gave us the feedback necessary to live out our strategies and fulfill our mission. Zero-balance budgeting provides all the feedback we need with an elegance and grace not often seen in the financial world.

One of the attributes that makes the zero-based budget so appealing to me is its flexibility. If you are budgeting to zero each month, your budget adjusts to whatever income you earn, because your spending is based upon your income. For some of you this might be a depressing thought ,considering your current situation. However, you might be surprised at how this kind of budgeting can help you keep your dignity, even when your finances feel as dry as the Sahara.

As you know, in the last seven years my financial situation has not exactly been a bowl of cherries. My income has dropped significantly but not steadily. I remember one particular budget which, when we wrote out all our usual expenses plus the extras for that month, came in $2,600 over our available income. That one took a while to sort out. It took us most of a drive between Seattle, Washington, and Portland, Oregon, to get the thing to work. I didn't want to make the necessary choices. I really wanted to just borrow money to make it through, but I had already learned my lesson on that little trap.

I really don't remember the final budget or how we finally got the thing together; what I do remember is the feeling of freedom when we did. It sticks out in my mind, because I was so shocked at our response to getting the thing done. Both my wife and I felt proud, almost elated, when both of us expected to feel sad and disheartened at the budget cuts. It is a feeling we have had from time to time over the last few years as we have made tight budgets work. It is a feeling of independence, of dignity, and empowerment, which you can't have if you choose to borrow money. If you value your independence and self-reliance, a successful zero-balance budget can make you feel good when the financial stress is at its worst. What else can I say? Zero-balance budgets are sexy.

Sexy or no, a budget is only as good as our follow-through. Isn't that where most of us fall down? We know what we want to do, but we end up doing something different with our limited money. One of those seductive luxury items whispers sweet nothings in our ear, and we instantly go all ADHD and forget everything we planned when we left home. Next thing you know, we are having to do some very fast talking to an irritated spouse. So how do we change this scenario? A simple method of following through on all our planning will be the subject of our next chapter.

Chapter 12:
How to Blow Wads of Cash and Love It

Plans are only as good as the follow-through. All the work we have done in the last two chapters is completely pointless unless we change our actual spending. Remember, our actual spending represents what we truly value at that moment in time. We may value something else one minute later, but we need to quit pretending it was someone else or some disease that made us make all those financially stupid choices. So the stakes are very high when we spend our money. If we do what we have always done, all the planning in the world won't matter. We will end up right back in the same place we always do, strapped for cash and feeling like a failure.

Many financial plans fall apart because they do not incorporate systems that guide actual spending. So how do we spend money in such a way it follows our zero-balance budget, guides us away from chasing status and toward stability? What we need is some kind of "stop spending" warning light that lets us know that we are approaching our budgeted limit for food or gasoline and we either need to redo the budget or wait until next month to make further purchases. Perhaps we could get a little red flashing light on our debit cards that told us when funds were low at the bank. Perhaps not: that would wreck one of the bank's major profit centers that comes from charging you overdraft fees.

Profit for the bank from your debit card doesn't only come from overdraft fees. Just using your debit card also creates another huge profit center for banks. Debit cards allow them to charge the merchants a processing fee. Guess who pays that fee in the form of higher prices? You do. So don't be fooled: even if you never overdraft your account, debit cards cost you money every time you use them. I really wish more merchants would do what both Arco gas stations and my barber does. Both of them charge me a small fee if I use my debit card. This allows me to make the choice of paying the fee or avoiding it by using cash.

Paper or Plastic?

Your bank has a vested interest in making sure that you continue to use some form of plastic for your spending. They make huge amounts of money when you do so. They also know something most of us don't know. Your spending habits deteriorate dramatically when you use *any* form of plastic to spend money. The social science is very clear on that topic. If you don't believe me, go look around on the internet. There are all sorts of media articles and studies you can read regarding spending habits and how debit cards cause us to buy impulse goods just as often as do credit cards. Your debit card is bad for your financial health, but it is a great way to make your bank profitable, so don't expect to see your bank helping you avoid the plastic in your wallet any time soon.

My current favorite media article on this topic appeared on the *Scientific American* website in July of 2011 under the title "Paying in Cash Keeps Us Healthy," which is probably a better title than mine which would have been "Yes, That Debit Card Does Make Your Butt Look Fat." The study showed there was no difference in impulse food shopping between those who used debit cards and those who used credit cards for their food purchases. However, those who spent cash on their food items were significantly more likely to avoid impulse food purchases, follow a shopping list, and purchase healthier foods overall. The scientists were surprised to see no difference between credit and debit cards. They assumed debit card users would hold back because debit card payments are immediately drawn from their accounts. Well, I guess they have never shopped with a debit card before.

This is only one of a group of studies that consistently show that when we spend cash, we make better choices with our money. Frankly, if you continue to use your debit card on a regular basis for everyday purchases like groceries, you might as well forget zero-balance budgeting or ever living a life of increasing financial stability. The science is just stacked too heavily against you. The vast majority of you will blow your budget with impulse purchases. In the world of financial stability, cash is king, and debit cards scream, "all the planning is done; now let's wreck it!"

Seeing Your Budget

So how does paper money keep us from impulse shopping when plastic cannot? For some of you, this will have to be one of those "try it to believe it" things, but when you do try it, you will see what a difference it makes. But most of us will get the idea, if we think through what happens with the typical budget at the end of the month.

Budgets are easy to manage for the first three weeks of the month, no matter how much you budgeted for any particular category of spending. It is the fourth week that becomes a problem. If I am spending my money using some form of plastic, chances are I will put in the cart the exact same things I put in the cart last week, including those fattening six packs and three quarts of Ben and Jerry's Cherry Garcia. I will go through the check-out line and not even know somewhere there is a bank executive shouting, "I smell a big fat bonus!" as another $35.00 overdraft fee gets added to my account.

On the other hand, if we have budgeted $425 to purchase food for our family of two, and we take it out in cash, as long as we keep it separate from all our other cash expenses, near the end of the month we will open the envelope and see we have $60.00 to last us for another five days until the next budget starts. In this case, we avoid the micro-brews, ice cream, and other luxury foods. We grab a few fresh things, some milk, bread, eggs, and a couple of other necessities, and walk out of the store to look in the freezer and figure out what we will eat for the next few days. Using cash changes the way we purchase goods and services, and we keep our banker from earning his insane bonus.

Please don't misunderstand; this is no cult of cash. I still use my debit card for certain purchases each month, but they are planned and accounted for in my zero-balance budget. For all one-time purchases, such as bills, I use online bill-pay systems or my debit card. However, for most spending categories in which money is spent throughout the month, I use cash. These include categories such as food, gasoline, clothing, household and personal products, and especially—entertainment and pocket money. I can't emphasize enough how important it is to use cash for the last two categories. More impulse purchases come from these two categories than any other. We need to make sure we can afford such purchases and make sure they do not hamper our ability to pay for our necessities. Spending only the cash we set aside for such purchases guarantees we do not break the budget with overspending.

At the beginning of the month, when we do our budget, my wife and I determine how much cash we will need to get out of our account. Then, once a month, we go to our local credit union and take our money out. (You do bank locally, don't you?) Once we have our cash, we divide it up between the categories we will fund with cash. We used to use envelopes for our various categories of cash, but recently we have found that we like using an accordion-style coupon folder. Keeping the cash in separate categories is important; it helps us know where to slow our spending, and where to take any extra money we need that month to meet our needs. It also helps us see our budget, and lets us make better decisions when we budget again next month.

For some of you, I know carrying around a month's worth of cash will be a hang-up, and it should be. We live in a pretty safe community, and we don't often carry all of it around with us. We will divide it in two and leave most of it at home. This will be necessary for some of you, depending where you live. I lived in Chicago for a couple of years, and there it was a totally different game. In that kind of place, you can bet I would never carry all my cash on me, at least not all in one place.

If you live in a place where carrying too much cash would make you feel unsafe, then once a month, take it out, divide it up into envelopes, and leave most of it in your home. This will keep you on track with your budget because your money has still been categorized. Then, either carry only a portion of it with you at any time, or carry a fixed amount which, depending on what you purchased, you replenish from the appropriate envelope when you get home. Besides, if you have built an emergency fund, you should be able to get by without having too much trouble even if you did have your money taken. I think that would count as an emergency.

Another thought here before I move along. If you are afraid that being mugged will cost you money and so are unwilling to use cash, consider how much money you spend in credit card interest charges each year. Which costs more? Honestly, even if I still lived in Chicago, I would carry cash and I would still save money over using credit cards even if I were robbed once a year, which is unlikely.

Earlier in the book, I talked about how I would teach you a feedback method that would instantly let you know if you need to adjust your budget. Well, I just taught it to you.

This instant feedback of your cash balance keeps small problems from becoming large and disastrous and helps you flex and change course. If you use cash for purchases, changing course and adjusting to unexpected expenses can be as simple as looking at your cash. If during the month the latest Middle-East crisis causes gasoline prices to spike, and you realize that you are going to have a problem, you simply look at your available cash and take some from another category in which you have a little to spare and put it in your gasoline category.

Remember the picture of you holding your monthly earnings in your hand as cash and looking out over a vast sea of possible goods and services? You didn't think I meant that literally, did you? I did.

Planning Your Cash Flow

One last thought on spending your money before we move on and conclude. My wife and I have been so dedicated to this idea of working on a monthly budget, we have managed to get ahead. That is, over time, we moved from paying this month's bills with this month's income to paying this month's bills with last month's income. This means when we sit down to budget, we look at our checking account to see what came in last month, and that is the money we spend this month on bills and expenses. For those of you with variable incomes, this will make your planning much easier. However, for many of you, you will not start out with this luxury. You are paying this month's bills with this month's income. This means, as you start out, you will need to manage your cash flow for the month carefully.

Approach your bills in the same way you approach your other spending. Pay your necessities first, and let the cable company wait for a paycheck later in the month. For a while you may need to take cash out twice a month, or you may decide to pay your bills from the first paycheck of the month and take your food and other cash items from the second paycheck. You can decide which way works best for you to manage your cash flow. Just be aware that over time, things are much simpler if you pay double on a bill occasionally to get ahead. Eventually you can work on a more solid foundation by simply spending what came in last month on the bills and expenses you have for this month. This provides some cushion and improves your financial stability by causing you to spend only money you have already earned, no more estimated commissions, just the amount that came in last month.

Liberation through Limits

When you take care of your necessities first, spending money can be quite liberating. When I was first learning these principles, I remember a Dave Ramsey fellow-traveler telling me about how much joy he and his family had while taking a vacation to Disneyland with cash. There was no hangover when they came home. He simply went back to work and kept moving forward. However, what amazed him most wasn't that he didn't feel guilty when he came home, it was how much fun he and his family had on the trip.

Sure, they had to make some tough decisions. They packed their own food and drove down instead of flying (west coast folks). They had to make some decisions along the way about what they wanted to do with their limited resources because they could not afford to do everything they wanted to do. However, they involved their children in those choices, and the family made them together. What made it so great for him is that he didn't have to sweat spending the money, like he usually did on a vacation paid for with a credit or debit card. He knew that every expense had been accounted for before they left.

Previously, when they traveled on a credit card, both he and his wife were afraid of every purchase they put on the card because they knew they couldn't pay for all of their spending when they got home. It wrecked all the fun because he felt anxious about the money the whole time he was away. Not a great way to relax on vacation, eh? Why doesn't he just take his smart phone along and answer all his work emails every day? (You do that on vacation? Seriously?) However, when he budgeted for his cash vacation, he had much more fun even though he was making more decisions and limiting his choices based on his money. He was freer to be himself because he only purchased what he could afford, and it made him a better dad because he was less worried and irritable. He found he greatly increased the value of his vacation through financial limits.

Putting limits on your spending and changing the way you spend money doesn't just help with big items. I remember what it was like not so long ago when my wife and I would go shopping for groceries. We would go with some kind of vague idea of what we had available for groceries for the week; we tended to use that quickie math system I talked about earlier, in which you simply subtract the bills from whatever is in the checking account and spend the rest. The problem was, we never knew just how much we had to spend. This would lead to lots of little squabbles as we shopped. She would put a block of cheese in the cart, and I would worry that we were spending the money we needed to set aside for the power bill or pay overdraft fees. I would put a six pack of micro-brew in the cart, and she would just shake her head no. (What can I say? I'm a beer snob.) Inevitably we would end up in a crunch, because we had spent the power bill or received an overdraft notice, and the accusations would fly, "Well if only you hadn't..."

The funny thing is, these fights seemed to magically disappear when we started living off a zero-balance budget. I trust my wife; I really do. And if she thinks we can afford that block of cheese or steak, then you won't hear me saying anything. I don't worry about what we spend on groceries and other items throughout the month, because I know that the electric bill has already been accounted for in our budget. Spending cash has been absolutely wonderful for creating trust in our relationship. For us, getting our priorities right and focusing our efforts on taking care of our basic needs first has paid both huge financial and personal dividends. Accepting limits, articulating them, and living within them, has truly made what has been a difficult seven years into something not only tolerable but worth celebrating. I cannot wait to see what our future holds.

Conclusion: Putting the Pieces Together

Book length ideas can be difficult to remember. Often there are too many useful nuggets to be able to hold on to all of them and my brain says, "Chuck it all!" and forgets everything, or I end up remembering just a few bits and pieces. I really don't want that to happen in this case. Wrapped up in the persuasion, asides, and ridiculous opinions are a few essential arguments which tie the chapters of this book together, and if you are willing to implement them, they provide a guide to surviving financial rough times.

Time and again, I have watched families who need to change the way they live become overwhelmed with everything they are supposed to *do* and fail to make any changes at all. They often do not realize the problem is not so much what they are doing but rather what they are thinking. Frequently for these families, it just feels easier to give up and allow the financial crisis they have created to take its course. In the short term it seems to work, and it is much easier. Unfortunately, if you abdicate your responsibility to live your own life, there really is no out for your humanity. Once you give in, you end up in a cycle of financial failure, which if taken to an extreme can destroy your ability to act independently. It has effects that last generations. I know, I have seen the damage such thinking can do to families. I have seen it in my own extended family.

In my counseling, after observing such defeatist thinking, I began to use the classic military model of war planning to help organize my advice into something more than useful nuggets. It provided a strong hook on which to hang our thinking about financial matters. Thinking this way helped me to put all the pieces together in my own life and organize my activity toward a goal that made sense. Making sense of the whole plan has helped me keep going when I wanted to quit. Each dollar I held in my hand now had a purpose. They existed to express my values. Suddenly, I had a defined mission and path to a financial goal that I could reach no matter what the economy threw at me.

Here then is a short summary of my financial plan. I hope it helps. If you follow it, I know what a difference it can make for you. I hope the information in this book helps you as much as it has helped me. I do make my living as a full-time writer and you can really help me out by writing a review of *How to Manage Your Money When You Don't Have Any* on its page on Amazon.com and if for some reason you got this book for free consider leaving me a tip in the tip jar on erikwecks.com. Thanks in advance for your thoughtful insights about my work and don't give up!

Your Financial Mission

To secure your basic needs both now and in the future, and to do nothing that would harm your ability to secure them on an ongoing basis.

Three Strategies to Accomplish Your Mission

1. Live below your means and save the rest for a rainy day.
2. If at all possible, live without using debt.
3. Follow a financial road map.

A Financial Road Map That Supports Your Mission

Step 0: On a monthly basis, make sure you are not spending more than you earn.
Step 1: Secure your basic needs: food, clothing and shelter.
Step 2: Create a $1,000 emergency fund.
Step 3: Pay off all debts as fast as possible, other than your home.
Step 4: Increase your emergency fund until it reaches 6 to 10 months of your basic needs.
Step 5: Begin saving 15 percent of your income for retirement.
Step 6: If so desired, save for your child's college education.
Step 7: Pay off your mortgage early.
Step 8: Express your values with your money.

Tactics That Bring Your Strategies to Life

Live by a zero-balance budget, created at least monthly.
Use cash whenever possible to avoid busting your budget

Workbook Available
May 15, 2015

HOW TO MANAGE

YOUR MONEY

WHEN YOU

DON'T HAVE ANY

——————— *Workbook* ———————

E R I K   W E C K S

Do You Live in an HOA?
Available Now

TRADE
HOA
STRESS

FOR
SUCCESS

RICHARD THOMPSON AND DOUG MCLAIN

WITH ERIK WECKS

Other Books and Stories

Erik Wecks' Published Books

Aetna Adrift
(A Pax Imperium Novel)
Grow up. Get answers. Get out.

Taylor's Watch
(A Pax Imperium Story)
Audra Taylor retired. The war had other plans.

He Dug the Grave Himself
(A Pax Imperium Story)
For fifty years Ephraim loved Lola, but did he really know her?

Brody: Hope Unconquered
(A Pax Imperium Novella)
Find a way to survive, no matter what the cost.

Unconquered
(A Pax Imperium Short Story Collection)
Tales of ordinary survival in extraordinary circumstances.

People for the Ethical Treatment of Robots
Lawrence Brudhomme is on a mission to take down Utopia.

Ruff
Gaark Mug Mug, neanderthal P.I., meet Frilly Twinklehearts, eccentric pink unicorn.

The Garden Between
Gardener Iorgas pours out his soul to tell Antipone that he loves her.

CPSIA information can be obtained
at www.ICGtesting.com
Printed in the USA
BVOW03s0624101216
470410BV00020B/1145/P